Lighten Up!

Lighten Up!

Confronting the darkness
with Christian character

Michael Shannon

with Jan Johnson

STANDARD
PUBLISHING
Cincinnati, Ohio

ISBN 0-7847-7068-9

Edited by Theresa C. Hayes
Cover design by Brian Fowler

The Standard Publishing Company, Cincinnati, Ohio.
A division of Standex International Corporation.

Introduction

Usually when someone tells us "lighten up," they are
admonishing us to relax, take it easy, or take things less seriously. That's not what we mean by the title of this book. We
are talking about letting our light shine before men
(Matthew 5:16). We are familiar with the Scripture that says
Jesus is the light of the world (John 8:12; 9:5). We would
never dispute that, but there is also a Scripture in which
Jesus tells us, "You are the light of the world" (Matthew
5:14-16). Is Jesus confused? Not at all. For both concepts
are true. Jesus is the light of the world and so are we. The
difference is that we are heirs of His reflected glory. We do
not generate the light; we let Christ's light shine through us.

A familiar illustration of this is the moon. The moon does
not generate light, but it effectively reflects the light of the
sun. In this study we will be looking at Jesus and other
Biblical characters and considering how they let their light
shine. We will see how God's light shines through our discipleship, willingness to share Christ with others, worship,
praise, and caring and sharing, and through our trust and
willingness to stand firm. These characters, with the excep-
tion of Jesus, are people like us. One of the reasons we like
role models is because they encourage us to do what they
do. Since we don't have to generate our own light, all of us
can be reflections of Christ's glory.

When George Bush was running for President, he called
Americans to volunteerism with the phrase, "A thousand
points of light." During his presidency he would give out

awards in the Thousand Points of Light Program. This is a beautiful image that Christians can adapt for use in the Kingdom of God. As each individual Christian bears the light of Christ, we can see there are millions of points of light.

It is our hope that after studying this series of lessons that you will be inspired by these saints of the past and that you can join them as one of God's "points of light."

One
You Light Up My Life

Jesus is the light of the world! Everything about Jesus shimmers like light: His life, His deeds, His teachings, His miracles, His exemplary behavior. He is a bright light that has invaded every dark corner of this world. There was even a time in Jesus' sojourn here on earth when He visibly shone before some of His disciples. This incident is called the transfiguration.

> After six days Jesus took with him Peter, James and John, the brother of James, and led them up a high mountain by themselves. There he was transfigured before them. His face shone like the sun, and his clothes became as white as the light. Just then there appeared before them Moses and Elijah, talking with Jesus.
>
> Peter said to Jesus, "Lord, it is good for us to be here. If you wish, I will put up three shelters—one for you, one for Moses and one for Elijah."
>
> While he was still speaking, a bright cloud enveloped them, and a voice from the cloud said, "This is my Son, whom I love; with him I am well pleased. Listen to him!"
>
> When the disciples heard this, they fell face down to the ground, terrified. But Jesus came and touched them. "Get up," he said. "Don't be afraid." When they looked up, they saw no one except Jesus.
>
> As they were coming down the mountain, Jesus instructed them, "Don't tell anyone what you have seen, until the Son of Man has been raised from the dead."
>
> Matthew 17:1-9

In the transfiguration, powerful use is made of light and a cloud. In the Old Testament, the Shekinah glory of God was represented by light and smoke. It's appropriate that Jesus is associated with light because light is a mystery. We can never fully understand it and we can never fully understand the nature of Christ.

Scientists today still discuss the nature of light. Sometimes it behaves as though it's made of particles, other times it behaves as though it's made of waves. We know that light can be so bright that we can see it from stars so far away that their distance can't be calculated. And yet light can also be as gentle as the night light in your house. The truth is that light is unique.

Light sustains life. There would be no life on this planet without it. Light is part of the essence of creation. Light is also a building block of this universe. Light has even been marshaled by physicians for surgery. Concentrate light into a laser and it can do amazing things. The military considers light a potential source for weaponry. Now we can send messages along beams of light. Yet, if we get too much of it, it can harm our bodies. So light is a mysterious thing in itself. For Jesus' face and garment to be radiating with light is mysterious, defying explanation and description. But it's here for us in God's inspired Word, which means there's something for us to learn from it.

Those who want easy answers would do well to avoid the account of the transfiguration. Jesus warned His disciples not to tell anybody about the experience until after the resurrection—and they didn't. That's because nobody would have believed them until after Jesus was resurrected from the dead. If you believe in the resurrection, the transfiguration is not hard to believe. But for those who don't believe in the resurrection, this event is unexplainable! Jesus did, however, share this with His inner circle—the three disciples He chose from the twelve. These three were a type of executive committee: Peter, James, and John.

Jesus brought them up to that mountain where He prayed,

but they fell asleep. When they awoke, they saw a wonderful thing: Jesus' face shining, Jesus' garment shining, Jesus talking with Moses and Elijah.

This must have had a tremendous impact on them, for John, in the opening of his Gospel, drew from the event. Speaking of Jesus, John wrote:

> Through him all things were made; without him nothing was made that has been made. In him was life, and that life was the light of men. The light shines in the darkness, but the darkness has not understood it.
>
> There came a man who was sent from God; his name was John. He came as a witness to testify concerning that light, so that through him all men might believe. He himself was not the light; he came only as a witness to the light. The true light that gives light to every man was coming into the world.
>
> John 1:3-9

Peter recalled the transfiguration as well in one of his epistles.

> We did not follow cleverly invented stories when we told you about the power and coming of our Lord Jesus Christ, but we were eyewitnesses of his majesty. For he received honor and glory from God the Father when the voice came to him from the Majestic Glory, saying, "This is my Son, whom I love; with him I am well pleased." We ourselves heard this voice that came from heaven when we were with him on the sacred mountain.
>
> And we have the word of the prophets made more certain, and you will do well to pay attention to it, as to a light shining in a dark place, until the day dawns and the morning star rises in your hearts.
>
> 2 Peter 1:16-19

The transfiguration had a great impact on both Peter and John. James was no doubt impressed too, but he didn't live long enough to write about it.

We come to this passage with a sense of reverence because the transfiguration is a strange and mysterious event. We may not get to see it with our physical eyes, but the splendor of Jesus still shines. He is the light of the world, and we can still capture a glimpse of that glory today and learn something from this incident.

*Flash*Points

1. When has light been a source of positive feelings for you? Negative feelings?

2. Why do you think light is an appropriate image for Jesus Christ?

3. In what ways has Jesus been a light in your life?

The Splendor of Jesus Commands Attention

Jesus cannot be ignored. While He was on earth, His true nature could not be restrained. When His divinity came shining through, these men were awed by it. Throughout time, sensible, open seekers of truth have not been able to overlook Jesus. That's why nearly every world religion tries to incorporate Jesus in some way into its system. For Peter, this particular event confirmed who Jesus was. About a week earlier, Simon Peter had said, "You are the Christ, the Son of the living God" (Matthew 16:16).

Even Jesus' enemies took notice, because He had a way of bringing out strong emotions. Even today, few people can read about Jesus and remain neutral. They either love Him or find Him troubling. Just as our eyes are sometimes uncomfortable in bright light, some people are uncomfortable in the presence of the light of Jesus. It's similar to the story about a little bat. "Help!" said the baby bat in his flight. "Turn on the dark, I'm afraid of the light." While most of us have experienced fear of the dark, some people are afraid of the light as well. They fear what the light will do to them. That's why Jesus cannot be ignored. The splendor of Jesus commands our attention.

*Flash*Points

1. This and subsequent pages will refer to the splendor of Jesus. What does the word, "splendor," mean to you?

2. Even though the three disciples knew Jesus well, they were stunned by His appearance. What would it take for you to be stunned by Jesus—especially if you've been a Christian for a while?

3. How do you suppose Jesus felt about the transfiguration event?

The Splendor of Jesus Fulfills Expectations

Historically, the Jews had longed for a messiah. The transfiguration stamps Jesus as the Messiah. This explains the presence of two important historical figures who had lived in great expectation of Jesus: Moses and Elijah. But why these two Old Testament figures? Was it because they both had significant encounters with God on a mountain? Moses went up to the mountain to get the law and came back with his face shining (Exodus 34:29-35). In despair, Elijah had a dramatic encounter with God on a mountain (1 Kings 19). But the similarity of mountain experiences is probably not the reason Moses and Elijah were present at the transfiguration.

Could the reason for their presence be that Moses and

Elijah had strange deaths? God took Moses' body and buried it himself (Deuteronomy 34:5, 6). Elijah was translated to glory in a chariot of fire (2 Kings 2:11). So they both had unusual endings to their lives. But that's probably not why they were present either. (As an aside, their presence on the mount of transfiguration is a comfort to all of us that our earthly death does not mean we cease to live. Moses and Elijah were alive and are alive now, even though they are no longer in their earthly bodies.)

These two figures show how Jesus fulfilled the expectation of both "the law and the prophets," a term people of Jesus' day frequently used when referring to the Old Testament (or old covenant). Who would represent the law better than Moses, the great law giver? And who would represent the prophets better than Elijah, the dramatic prophet? By then, Jesus had already emphasized, "Do not think that I have come to abolish the Law or the Prophets; I have not come to abolish them but to fulfill them" (Matthew 5:17). Jesus said His teachings were a continuation, or summary, of the law and the prophets. Jesus himself was the perfect embodiment of the law and He perfectly fulfilled it. He fulfilled the prophecies of the Old Testament as well. So meeting with Moses and Elijah on the mountain was a way to say that Jesus was the completion of the law and the prophets.

It's been noted that Moses and Elijah appeared in order to disappear. Their disappearance testified to the superiority of Jesus. As the King James Version words it: "And when they had lifted up their eyes, they saw no man, save Jesus only" (Matthew 17:8). That detail may be just a small item in the narrative, but many commentators, preachers, and poets have noted the appropriateness of Moses and Elijah disappearing. There alone stood Jesus, the perfect fulfillment of the law and the prophets. The splendor of Jesus satisfies the expectation of history. For many years people waited for God to intervene. They waited for the Messiah to come, and on that mountain that day God was saying, "He's here!"

*Flash*Points

1. Think of a time when you desperately wanted a certain person to show up. Use that kind of feeling and wording to describe how the Jews of that day longed for the Messiah to come.

2. In what ways did Jesus fulfill (complete, embody, satisfy) the law (for example, the Ten Commandments)?

3. In what ways did Jesus fulfill the prophets (for example, predictions of His birth and death, calling people to righteousness, announcing hope for the future)?

The Splendor of Jesus Prompts Reverence

The disciples were so reverent on this occasion that by the end of it, they were "afraid." Jesus even had to tell them to stand up and not be afraid. We can understand why they were afraid. They witnessed Jesus' radiant appearance, the cloud enveloping them, Moses and Elijah appearing, the voice of God speaking.

In our evangelism, we often try to emphasize that Jesus is a friend to sinners. And He is. One of the purposes of the incarnation was to make God more accessible to us through Christ. However, we ought not to rob God or rob Jesus of the reverence they deserve. Jesus is not just a buddy. He's the Lord and we ought to revere him. In our attempt to make Jesus user-friendly, we cannot forget that He sits enthroned at the right hand of the Father. This event certainly prompted reverence in the disciples, and it should prompt us to be reverent before our Lord Jesus Christ.

*Flash*Points

1. Of the descriptive details of the transfiguration, what would have been most frightening to you if you had been present?

2. What are some words that describe your feelings about Jesus having access to such other-worldly powers as talking to people who are dead, being able to exude unearthly light, and taking control of clouds?

3. What posture in prayer would be an appropriate one to show your reverence to God?

The Splendor of Jesus Encompasses Sacrifice

What were Moses and Elijah talking about? Matthew did not tell us, but Luke did. He said they were talking about Jesus' exodus or departure—actually, His death (Luke 9:31). It seems incongruous that at this eloquent moment of high drama they were discussing Jesus' impending death. You would think they wouldn't want the Messiah to die. Yet it's significant and appropriate that the Messiah would die for us. We are grateful that God cared enough for us to visit us at all on this earth. Beyond that, it's remarkable that Jesus would teach, heal, and then die for us. That's an incredible truth that we need to grasp. Far from diminishing the splendor of Jesus, His death enhances it. Calvary didn't take away Jesus' divinity. That the divine one was crucified on a cross as a common criminal only makes His light shine more. Peter himself didn't want Jesus to face this kind of death, but on that mountain that day, part of the glory of Jesus was His determination to fulfill His destiny on the cross of Calvary. The glory of Jesus is not the glory of someone who never tasted suffering. He was not a person to be always served, but a servant himself. That only makes Him shine even brighter!

$\mathcal{Flash}$**Points**

1. How does the death of Jesus enhance His splendor?

2. In what way is this statement true: "That the divine one was crucified on a cross as a common criminal only makes His light shine more."

3. In what ways has God called you to imitate Christ as one who serves instead of insists on being served?

The Splendor of Jesus Demands Our Obedience

Peter was so excited about the transfiguration that he said, "If you wish, I will put up three shelters—one for you, one for Moses and one for Elijah." At that point, a great cloud enveloped them and the voice of God said, "This is my Son, whom I love. . . . Listen to him" (Matthew 17:4, 5). The literal translation is, "Keep on listening to him."

What did Peter have in mind? Why did God interrupt Peter's idea? In the King James Version, the word used in Peter's suggestion was that three "tabernacles" be built. And since we think of the Old Testament place of worship as a tabernacle, some think Peter was suggesting that they worship Moses, Elijah, and Jesus equally. But the word "tabernacle" means tent, booth, or lean-to. It's a temporary dwelling place. So Peter wasn't saying he wanted to worship all three equally. But what was he saying? Whatever it was, the abrupt shift of events implies that his suggestion was not a wise one.

What is certain is that Peter didn't want that moment to end. And if you've ever had a high spiritual moment, you know how he felt. You want to stay in the clouds instead of going down the valley. But in the valley, people are hurting. When Jesus and the three disciples came down from that mount of transfiguration, they found waiting for them a man with a sick son, needing the healing hand of Jesus. Also waiting for them was the cross of Calvary yet to come. But Peter didn't want to go down there. He wanted to stay at that high moment as long as he could. But the truth is that we have those high moments to prepare us to go to the valley and meet the needs of others.

Years ago when I was a college student on a camp team, I served at a camp where vespers services were held high up on the hill in the late afternoon. At this service, people spontaneously testified, and so this one hour service might turn into a three hour service. Once, we actually missed our supper because nearly every camper had given some sort of testimony. In the closing prayer circle that night, the leader said, "I think it's time for us to go off this hill back down to the valley. What would have happened to Jesus and Peter, James, and John if they had stayed on the mountain?" The camper next to me leaned over and whispered, "They would have starved to death."

There is a time to get off the mountain and to meet the needs of others. We can't lose sight of the hurting people in the world. In our world, there will also be a road that leads to Calvary. In spite of Peter's objection, there will be a cross and death. There will be darkness at midday. And there will even be some people who think they have snuffed out that light forever. They couldn't be more wrong. For we know that the light reemerges stronger than ever. From Calvary, the eternal light and life of Christ shines more brightly than ever before.

*Flash*Points

1. Describe a mountaintop experience you've had.

2. How do you make a space in your life for regular close-up encounters with God?

3. What does it mean for us that Peter, James and John did not go down off the mountain by themselves, but Jesus walked beside them?

The Splendor of Jesus Still Shines Today

What does the transfiguration mean to us today? I read a commentator who answered this question by saying, "Not much really." Not much? If it wasn't important, why would it be recorded in the Bible? We might as well ask what the resurrection has to do with us today or what the second coming has to do with us today. The transfiguration is important to us today for several reasons.

First, we learn from this event that our inner nature will eventually shine through. What we are will be made known. Sometimes a crisis is what makes our character visible. If there is any light in us during a crisis, we know it comes from Jesus.

Someone has said there are only two ways to spread light—either be the candle or be a mirror that reflects the candle. Jesus is the light and we are the mirrors that reflect the light. Jesus is like the sun that produces light and we are like the moon that reflects that light. A simple reflection sounds like a small thing, but it's not. Many people in this world would never have known Jesus without the reflected glory they saw in Christians.

But this passage is not about us; it's about Jesus. His transfiguration also tells us that Jesus really is who He said

He was. He really is divine. He really is the light of the world. If we pay attention to Jesus, understand His relationship to the Old Testament promises, understand the importance of being reverent before Him, understand what He did for us at Calvary, and decide to make Him Lord of our lives, then we can say to Him, "Jesus, you light up my life." And as He lights up our lives we, in turn, can light the way for others.

As the poet Goethe faced the end of his life, his last words were, "More light." I don't know exactly what Goethe meant, but that's a cry we hear from many people today. They're out in this dark world saying, "Light. More light." In Jesus' day, it was such a dark world that the transfigured Christ was a dramatic vision for them. In fact, that word, "transfigure," is the word that gives us our English word, "metamorphosis." When we use the term metamorphosis, we think of an ugly caterpillar turning into a beautiful butterfly. This dramatic, outward change came from an inward dynamic. It was as if Jesus' nature could no longer be held in by His flesh. And His disciples saw Him as the bright and shining Lord that He is.

One of my favorite writers is O. Henry. I enjoy how he always had a little twist to his stories and how he was always interested in the lives of common people and their struggles. When William Sydney Porter (O. Henry's real name) passed away, his last words to his nurse were: "Mary, pull up the shades. I don't want to go home in the dark." Who does? I don't. I don't think you do either. None of us wants to go home in the dark. Thanks to the light of Christ and its reflected glory in countless disciples, none of us needs ever fear going home in the dark.

*Flash*Points

1. Since we're reflectors of Christ's glory (and not genera-
   tors of light ourselves), what important things can we do
   to be adequate reflectors of that glory?

2. The author says that you can say to Jesus, "Jesus, you
   light up my life," if you do the following:
   a. pay attention to Jesus;
   b. understand His relationship to the Old Testament
      promises;
   c. understand the importance of being reverent before
      Him;
   d. understand what He did for you at Calvary;
   e. make Him Lord of your life.

   Rate the above items 1-5 according to your need to do
   them. Mark a 1 by the thing you need to do most.

3. Consider the words, "An outward change comes from an
   inward dynamic." What outward change is needed in
   your life? What inward dynamic has to be in place in
   order for that to happen?

Two
Sharing the Light

Jesus was frequently invited for dinner and He usually accepted the invitation. The Gospels record many of these events for us. Jesus was a guest at the home of Mary and Martha and Lazarus, He dined in the homes of at least three different Pharisees, He visited the home of Zacchaeus, and He shared meals with His disciples before His resurrection and after. Of all these, no dinner had a more bizarre guest list than the dinner with Matthew.

Matthew's first act as a disciple was to invite his friends over to his house to meet Jesus. Matthew was a tax collector and was therefore considered by most to be a traitor and a thief. Some of the people he invited to dinner were also tax collectors, and the rest of his guests were equally considered by the Pharisees to be "sinners." What kind of sinners they were, we have no way of knowing, but the Pharisees were outraged that Jesus would socialize with people of this type.

*Flash*Points

1. Imagine this scene if it occurred today. What disreputable people might be invited to a dinner party thrown by a criminal?

2. What does Matthew's willingness to invite his friends tell us about his relationship with Jesus?

3. In what ways is Jesus asking you to take your call to discipleship more seriously?

The Pharisees were standing by, heckling Matthew's guests as they dined. These esteemed Jewish leaders would not, of course, have joined those at the table and they criticized Jesus for doing so. They also busied themselves asking Jesus' disciples a question, "Why does your teacher eat with tax collectors and sinners?"

That's the question before us today. Why indeed? Why did Jesus accept such invitations? Why did Matthew issue such an invitation? To Matthew, the invitation was probably a natural outgrowth of his own gratitude or a simple response to Jesus' words that He came "to seek and to save that which was lost" (Luke 19:10, KJV). Maybe Matthew invited these people because he had compassion for them. Whatever his reasons, Matthew seemed to view the dinner as perfectly normal.

Some would argue that Christians today need to separate themselves from the world, but if you take that too far, how would any new conversions ever be made? We should separate ourselves from the world in the sense that we don't buy into the world's system, the world's priorities, or the world's values. But even as we deny these worldly things, we must reach out to the world and take the gospel to its people.

*Flash*Points

1. What criticisms might Jesus receive today if He attended a dinner party where the other guests were thought to be notorious sinners?

2. Which of these systems, priorities, and values of the world do you find most deadly?
   •watching out for #1 (and #1's family)
   •being greedy and materialistic
   •staying busy and hurrying
   •taking what isn't mine
   •ignoring those in need
   •disrespecting others
   •focusing on self
   •self-promotion
   •using others

3. Who was the last person to "sit at your table" or whom you invited to go with you somewhere? Whom would you like to invite next?

4. What kinds of things prompt your compassion for the
   lost?

We are all sinners—some are just "more acceptable" sinners than others! Some sins may not be as obvious as others,
but no one is without sin. In the classic television series, "All
in the Family," Archie Bunker was difficult to live with but
his wife, Edith, was a very sweet person. In one scene, Archie
got mad at her for being so good. He said to her, "That's you,
all right! Edith the good! You'll stop at nothing to be good.
You never make nobody mad! Do you think it's easy living
with a saint? Even when you cheat, you don't cheat to win.
You cheat to lose! Edith, you ain't human!" To which Edith
said, "That's a terrible thing to say, Archie Bunker. I'm just as
human as you are!" Archie replied, "Oh yeah? Then prove
you're just as human as me—do something rotten!"

Unlike Edith, most of us don't have to be urged to do
something rotten. Most of us find that rottenness comes pretty naturally to us! Because sin is so easy for us to fall into,
we can't consider ourselves superior or inferior to anybody
else. The ease with which we fall into sin is illustrated in a
little verse called "Sweet Peril" by George MacDonald, who
was one of C.S. Lewis' influences.

> Alas, how easily things go wrong!
> A sigh too much, or a kiss too long,
> and there follows a mist and a weeping rain,
> And life is never the same again.

We know this to be true from experience. Many people
suffer the rest of their lives for a decision made in a second.

*Flash*Point

1. If you were writing a verse like MacDonald's today, what sin would you describe in line two that reflects your own particular weakness (e.g., pride, greed, gluttony)? Can you express it succinctly, as he did?

A _____ too _____.

In Jesus' response to the questions and barbs of the Pharisees we can find three vivid images of sinners. These images will help us today as we view others and ourselves. Too often, we view "sinners" as the enemy instead of victims of the enemy. So Jesus gave us these pictures to help us.

• **The sick.** "It is not the healthy who need a doctor, but the sick." In making that statement, Jesus suggested that sinners are sick people who need a cure.

• **The guilty.** Jesus instructed the Pharisees, the disciples, and us to value mercy over sacrifice. Sinners are guilty people in need of a pardon.

• **The hungry.** Finally, Jesus said He'd come to call sinners, not the righteous. The word for "call" is the word normally used to mean "invite," such as to invite someone to your house. When you combine that with the setting of Jesus around the table with these "sinners," He seems to be suggesting that sinners are hungry people in need of sustenance.

If we examine how Jesus looked at sinners, we will see how we should look at sinners. Matthew, no doubt, wanted to share the light with others. He saw himself as someone who wanted to be a "night light" for those who were walking around in darkness.

*Flash*Points

1. Think of someone you know who needs Christ. In what way is he or she sick? Guilty? Hungry?

2. Jesus was good at looking into people's hearts and seeing their sickness, guilt, and hunger. What would help you care more about what is in a person's heart?

3. Of Jesus' three images of sinners (sick, guilty, hungry), which one fits you best?

Sick People Who Need a Cure

When Jesus said "It is not the healthy that need a doctor, but the sick," He was offering himself as the great physician to help people with this sickness called sin. And when you're sick, how do you feel? If nothing else, you feel uncomfortable. You don't feel like getting up. When you try, you feel dizzy and don't have the energy you once had. The only thing you feel like doing is sitting.

Sin makes us feel uncomfortable, too. Some people appear to be having a good time but at the core, they feel discomfort with their sinful lifestyle. They know that they're not living up to their best. Both sickness and sin keep us from being effective. When hampered by sickness, we don't think as we would normally think. Our reactions aren't as fast. We don't drive as well. We don't do our work very well.

Likewise, sin keeps us from reaching our ultimate potential. Left unattended, sin can lead us into danger just as untreated sickness can make us seriously ill. Your sickness might be a small thing, but if you don't get treatment and find healing, it can lead to death. Even a small cut, if infected and untreated, can lead to death. Sin works the same way. Some sins seem small, but when left unattended, they eventually lead to death.

*Flash*Points

1. In what other ways, if any, are sickness and sin similar?

2. For what reasons do we leave our sin "untreated"?

3. How does sin, in general, keep the world from being efficient and caring?

4. What do we need to do to "attend" to our sin?

Guilty People Who Need Mercy

Sinners are guilty people who need mercy and pardon. Jesus said, "I desire mercy, not sacrifice" (Matthew 9:13). When Jesus said this, He quoted from the book of Hosea, one of my favorite Old Testament books. It includes the story of the prophet, Hosea, who was told by God to go back and reclaim his wife who had gone off into prostitution and slavery. Interestingly, Hosea did go and buy her back. He paid money to bring her back home. This sounds a lot like what Jesus did for us.

Only guilty people need mercy. However, since we're all sinners and all guilty, we all need mercy. Some of us pretend that we're not guilty of anything, but we know inside that we are. We're like the fellow who was put on trial for robbing a bank. His attorney was good and presented an excellent case. The accused waited nervously for the jury's decision. When the jury returned and announced, "Not guilty," the man jumped up and down excitedly and asked his attorney, "Does this mean I get to keep the money?" We know we're at fault.

As guilty people, we're in need of a pardon. Guilty people don't have any real freedom. They're always looking over their shoulder because they're chained to their sins and desires. When they're pardoned, though, it's as if they never committed the wrong. All rights and privileges are restored. They can know true freedom.

In our guilt we don't have any real hope of ever living a life of peace again. But once we're pardoned, we're treated as if we had never sinned. Guilty people never know what it's like to really feel clean. I've counseled with people who have said, "I just feel so dirty." But a pardon wipes that away. We're considered totally clean.

Consider Carla Faye Tucker. She was led into a life of prostitution and drug addition when she was a young woman. This eventually led her to brutally murder two people with a pickax. Before Carla Faye Tucker was put to death with a lethal injection, many people pleaded that her sentence be commuted to life in prison without parole. People such as Pat Robertson—and even the Pope—spoke up for her. Many people who visited this articulate, sweet woman, or saw her on television couldn't imagine that she was the same person who committed those murders.

Carla Faye Tucker claimed to have found Christ in prison and I have no reason to dispute her claim. That meant she was not the same person in the Lord's eyes. If her repentance was sincere and her conversion was real, then regardless of how her life ended, she knew the peace that comes from receiving the mercy of the Father. If there is hope for the Carla Faye Tuckers of the world, then there's hope for us.

Maybe it bothers you to think that you may see murderers in Heaven. But you could turn that idea around and think, "If God's mercy covers them, it is surely covers me." Romans 5:20, 21 conveys the marvelous truth that God's grace is greater than all our sins.

I heard a wonderful story years ago. Two brothers in the old West rustled cattle and stole sheep for a living. They were finally captured, jailed, and convicted. With a sense of frontier justice, the judge gave them two choices: they could leave the town for good, or stay and accept their punishment. That punishment was to be branded forever as sheep thieves. One of the brothers decided to leave town, but the other brother was in love with a young lady in town. He decided to stay and accept his punishment.

The brands were heated red hot and an "S and a "T" were seared on his forehead, the letters standing for "sheep thief." His scar stared people in the face every day, but the man made the most of his opportunity for a new life. He began going to church. He courted the young lady and eventually married her and had a family. He became one of the leading citizens of the community, known for his charity and good will. When people moved to town, they would sometimes ask about the man. One newcomer said, "He seems like such a nice fellow I hate to ask him what that ST brand on his forehead stands for. Why does he have those letters there?" Someone replied, "Well, I'm not sure, but I think it's an abbreviation for the word, 'saint.'" Our God is the kind of God who can take sheep thieves and turn them into saints.

*Flash*Points

1. In what ways did Hosea reflect the heart of God?

2. What aspect of the story of the sheep thief turned charitable townsman was most meaningful to you?

3. Consider honestly whose presence in Heaven would bother you. Then say a few times, "If God's mercy extends to _____, then it surely extends to me."

Hungry People in Need of Sustenance

Among the basic needs for food, water, shelter, and clothing, only thirst is more urgent than hunger. When you're hungry, you can't think about anything else. If people are hungry enough, they'll do desperate things—even scavenge in trash cans.

People will also do desperate things to meet their spiritual hunger. They may turn to food, alcohol, sex, drugs, gambling, or cults to try to fill the void in their lives. However, like drinking salt water to get rid of your thirst, these things only make spiritual hunger worse.

Others make matters worse for themselves by not admitting that they're sinners. It is interesting to note that these are often the very people who are quick to point out the sin in other people's lives! Have you noticed how there is always someone in your life who is willing to point out your sins for you? In Charlie Brown's life, that person is Lucy, who sets up her little roadside psychiatric stand. One particular "Peanuts" cartoon strip showed Lucy giving counsel to Charlie Brown. She said, "Sometimes I feel that we are not communicating. You, Charlie Brown, are a foul ball in the line drive of life. You're often in the shadow of your own goal post. You are a miscue. You're a three putt on the eighteenth green. You are a seven-ten split in the tenth frame. You are a dropped rod and reel in the lake of life. You're a missed free throw. You're a shanked nine iron. A called third strike. A bug on the windshield of life. Do you understand? Have I made myself clear?"

Charlie Brown isn't that bad. Maybe you're not that bad either, but the painful reality is that we are sinners.

The problem the Pharisees had with Jesus was that He shared a table with tax collectors and other sinners. He was, in fact, showing affection for them! He had compassion for them. That was Jesus' mission—to seek and to save those who are lost. We are all hungry people in need of sustenance from the Lord. But if hungry people don't come to the table, not only do they not get the food they need, but they never know real fellowship either. Today, as in Jesus' day, the sharing of a meal is an occasion for fellowship. Matthew brought his friends to the table with Jesus as part of his discipleship. We need to invite those in the world to join us at the table. After all, that's how we got into fellowship with Jesus!

*Flash*Points

1. What helps people admit their sin when they've been overlooking it or finding it difficult to acknowledge?

2. When we don't know Christ, what are we hungering for and not finding?

3. In what ways is God calling you to share Jesus' mission—to be compassionate and rub elbows with the lost?

A little girl answered the phone in her house and a salesman said, "Little girl, may I speak to your mother?" The little girl replied, "She's busy right now."

The salesman said, "Oh, OK. How about your father?" The little girl replied that he was busy too, so the salesman asked if she had any brothers and sisters. She told him she had one brother and one sister. He asked to speak to one of them, but she said they were busy too. "Wow," the salesman observed, "everybody seems busy at your house. What are they all busy doing?"

"Oh," she replied, "they're all looking for me."

That's what we ought to be busy doing—looking for those who need the gospel. We need to be looking for those sick people who need a cure, for those guilty people who need a pardon, and for those hungry people who need sustenance.

Those who are lost also have several responsibilities. They must submit themselves to the great physician in order to receive the cure. They must accept the pardon. They must

RSVP the invitation. Some sinners think they don't belong at the table fellowshiping with Jesus, but they do. And it is our responsibility to issue that invitation and pray that they'll come to take their place at the table.

Three
The Guiding Light

Have you ever read stories of the great saints of the Bible and said to yourself, "I could never be like them. They are so much more talented than I. They have a much higher level of commitment and spirituality."

The person I'd like to bring to your attention is an "every-man" figure. He's a person we could all be like—a simple man named Andrew. What do we know about Andrew? We know he was a fisherman and was Simon Peter's brother. These two brothers were from Bethsaida, which was a great town for fishermen. Bethsaida means "house of fishermen." Peter and Andrew were part of a fishing business in Capernaum and they were disciples of John. ("John" in this passage refers to John the Baptist.)

Andrew was a devout Jew—one who hoped for the Messiah. Andrew's name means "manly," which fits a fisherman and an outdoorsman. He could relate to the outdoor lifestyle, strange clothes, and unusual food of John the Baptist.

In John 1:35-42 we find a picture of Andrew, a disciple of John the Baptist, and his first encounter with Jesus:

> The next day John was there again with two of his disciples. When he saw Jesus passing by, he said, "Look, the Lamb of God!"
> When the two disciples heard him say this, they followed Jesus. Turning around, Jesus saw them following and asked,

"What do you want?"

They said, "Rabbi" (which means Teacher), "where are you staying?"

"Come," he replied, "and you will see."

So they went and saw where he was staying, and spent that day with him. It was about the tenth hour.

Andrew, Simon Peter's brother, was one of the two who heard what John had said and who had followed Jesus. The first thing Andrew did was to find his brother Simon and tell him. "We have found the Messiah" (that is, the Christ). And he brought him to Jesus.

Jesus looked at him and said, "You are Simon son of John. You will be called Cephas" (which, when translated, is Peter).

Andrew is an example of one who was willing to be a witness and a guiding light for someone else. We remember Simon Peter and his eloquence, but apparently Andrew was not eloquent. We remember Simon Peter's boldness, but apparently Andrew was not bold. He was, however, the first disciple of Jesus.

*Flash*Points

1. With whom do you identify more—Andrew or Simon Peter?

2. When was the last time you called your siblings or relatives to tell them about a "good deal"?

We can learn from Andrew how to be that quiet witness, that gentle persuader, that guiding light. If we're going to lead others to the Lord, we need to observe the following principles.

We Need to Get Clear About Our Own Convictions

Andrew developed his convictions first from John the Baptist, who taught him the need for repentance and baptism. John planted the seeds of discipleship in Andrew's life. But when his teacher said Jesus was the "Lamb of God" (v. 36), Andrew went to investigate for himself. Andrew and another of John's disciples followed Jesus until Jesus turned around, looked at them and said, "What do you want?" Literally, this means, "What do you seek? What are you looking for?"

With this one question, Jesus asked Andrew to search his heart. What was he looking for in a messiah? Was he looking for a political messiah to drive out the Romans? Was he looking for a legalistic messiah who would join forces with the Pharisees? Was he looking for a personal messiah who would simply help him deal with his problems? Was he looking for a messiah who would give him a place of honor and power and influence? What sort of messiah are you looking for? That's a question all of us have to answer.

Andrew and the other follower answered Jesus' question with a question of their own, "Where are you staying?" Jesus invited them to come and see. Andrew spent that day talking with Jesus, listening to Him teach, and developing some convictions. When Andrew went back to find Peter, his message was simple: "We have found the Messiah" (v. 41). He didn't say, "I think possibly, maybe, we might have found a potential messiah candidate." He was sure he'd found the Messiah.

If we want to be a guiding light like Andrew, we have to begin with our own convictions. If we don't believe something, there is nothing for us to share. Yet, to be clear about our convictions doesn't mean that we won't ever ask questions or have doubts. It does mean that we will commit ourselves to study, learn, grow, and strengthen our convictions. Can I prove to you beyond a shadow of a doubt that God exists? No, although I am certain of it. Can I prove to you beyond a shadow of a doubt that Jesus is God's Son? No, although I am certain of it. So even though you may question, you can still develop convictions, as Andrew did.

*Flash*Points

1. About what issues of faith do you have questions and doubts?

2. Who would be a helpful person to discuss these with?

3. About what points of faith do you feel a great deal of conviction?

We Can't Be Afraid to Share the Gospel With Those Close to Us

The first thing that came to Andrew's mind was to share this message with his brother Simon. A lot of people today are reluctant to witness to their own family for a number of reasons. They think, "Maybe that will change the dynamics of our relationship, or perhaps they will reject me." And sometimes that happens, but not always. Others think, "If I witness to my family and friends, they'll think I've become an obnoxious nag." That could happen, too, but doesn't have to.

Some years ago, I heard a preacher talk about a time when he was a revival speaker and went calling with the host minister. They went to a house to witness and the woman who met them at the door was smoking. The host minister didn't like smoking, so he said, "Woman, get that wicked weed out of your mouth and maybe we'll talk to you about Jesus."

Somehow the revival speaker managed to turn the visit around to something positive. When they got back in the car, he said to the host minister, "If you ever do that again, I will never visit with you again. I don't care what you think about her habit. She's a precious soul and that was her home. We were intruding in her space and you were rude." So it is possible that Christians in their excitement may be obnoxious, but they don't have to be.

There are abundant reasons why we should be interested in taking the gospel to our family and friends. If you really care about those closest to you, you'll want them to find what you've found. That's the way the gospel has always worked. Leslie Flynn, in his book, *The Twelve,* tells about a man in a restaurant who was seated next to a big picture window. Outside, a shabbily dressed little boy peered into the restaurant, licking his lips. The man was so moved that he went outside and asked the boy, "Are you hungry?"

"Sure am," replied the boy. So the man brought the boy

inside and let him order from the menu. But when the food
was delivered to the table, the boy wouldn't eat it. "I thought
you were hungry," said the man.

"Sure am," said the boy.

"Then why don't you eat?"

The little boy pointed outside to another dirty face
pressed up against the window. He said, "That's my little
brother. How can I eat with him standing there and looking
at me like that?" So you know what the man did. He went
out and brought the other boy in and served both of them
some food. That boy's feeling of wanting to share a meal
with his hungry brother is the same kind of feeling Andrew
had for Peter: "I have found the Messiah and I want you to
find him too!"

In circles where church growth is studied, people talk
about "the web" or the "network principle." They're referring to the fact that people are usually won by their close
friends or family. One church conducted a study, asking people, "How did you get here?" They found that in one five
year period, more than twenty-five people had come to the
Lord because of one person.

When I first learned of this principle, I decided to examine
it in my own Sunday school class. The class I was teaching
at the time had about thirty-five students. I asked them,
"How did you get to this church?" They started telling their
stories and we found only two couples in that class had not
been invited by somebody else—one was my wife and me
and we had been hired to come there. Nearly all of them
came because close friends or family had invited them.

This principle works. Look at Jesus' twelve disciples.
They include at least three brother teams: Peter and Andrew,
James and John, Matthew and James the Less. Some believe
Philip and Bartholomew were brothers, but we don't know
for sure. So at least half the disciples were brothers. There
may also have been a father and son team. One of the twelve
was called, literally "Judas son of James" (Luke 6:16 in the
New International Version). The *King James Version* says,

"Judas, brother of James" but the word "brother" is not in the original text. It says simply, "Judas of James." Normally we would take that to mean "son of." So the disciples may have included a father and son team. No doubt, many of them were friends and acquaintances. Peter, Andrew, James, and John worked side by side in the same business, and over on the shore was Matthew, who sat at the tax collecting booth (Matthew 9:9).

Friends and family have always brought each other into the kingdom—no matter how nervous or uncomfortable they were about it. Normally we win people in our own circle of family and friends.

*Flash*Points

1. What fears do you have about being obnoxious when sharing your faith?

2. What attitudes and character qualities did the revival speaker have that helped him avoid being obnoxious?

3. In what ways is respect important when sharing our
   faith?

If we want to make sure we're not becoming that obnoxious Christian, we need to observe the third principle.

We Can't Argue People Into the Kingdom

When Andrew first went to Simon Peter, he simply said,
"We have found the Messiah." Then he beckoned Peter to
come and meet Jesus. He didn't get into a debate over the
nature of the Messiah. He didn't bring out the messianic
texts in the Old Testament. He simply said, "We found Him.
Check it out for yourself." If that's your approach, not many
people will be offended.

It's characteristic of Andrew that whenever we see him in
Scripture, he is inviting somebody to meet Jesus. Before
Jesus fed the crowd of five thousand men, plus their families, all these people were listening to Jesus teach. The day
wore on and they got hungry, but there was no nearby place
to buy food. One boy had a lunch, and guess who introduced
him to Jesus? Andrew.

On another occasion Greek-speaking folks heard of Jesus
and wanted to meet Him. They went to Andrew. Andrew
introduced them to Jesus. Andrew may have been a one-
talent person, but he used that one talent well. Maybe you
think your contribution to the kingdom isn't great, but it
may be greater than you think. If you're doing a job that
doesn't get a lot of notice or acclaim, you can still use your
talent for God's glory as Andrew did.

*Flash*Points

1. In what ways can we invite others to "check it out for yourself" regarding the gospel?

2. At what point do our requests become pushy or argumentative?

Don't Be Afraid to Take a Back Seat

In the synoptic Gospels of Matthew, Mark, and Luke, the only time Andrew is mentioned is in the list of apostles. Only the Gospel of John tells us anything more about Andrew. Some people believe that the other disciple mentioned in John 1:35-40 was John. That may be, because John was hesitant to mention himself in his Gospel. And if that's the case, it's interesting that when he wrote his Gospel, John made sure Andrew was not left out.

In the early part of Jesus' ministry, Andrew seems to have been part of the inner circle, but by the time of transfiguration, he was not. The only disciples present for this glorious event were Peter, James, and John. Yet we find no indication that Andrew resented or was angry about missing this occasion. He seemed simply to accept his particular part in the work of the kingdom.

Andrew also took a back seat at Pentecost when Peter was the one who preached the gospel message. Peter delivered that great sermon and three thousand people responded. Andrew won one person while Peter won three thousand in one day. Do you suppose Andrew sat in the corner, saying, "I can't believe it! That's my brother. He's not more talented than I am. I don't understand this." Or did he say, "Boy, if they only knew my brother the way I know him, they wouldn't be so impressed"? We don't know what Andrew thought, but there's no indication that it bothered him to take that back seat.

People often give Simon Peter "credit" for those three thousand conversions. (Of course, all the credit for conversions goes to God.) But if you trace back the sequence of events, Andrew was responsible. Andrew won Peter, and Peter won the three thousand with his preaching. Andrew did his part, and his influence was very significant!

Still, throughout history, Andrew has been overshadowed by others. When people go to Rome to visit the Vatican, they go to the church named St. Peter's, not St. Andrew's. Is there a St. Andrew's? If there is, I don't know where. So even in history, Andrew fades from the scene.

There are, however, a few things named after St. Andrew. One is in our country, but we don't notice it right away because it's named in a different language. In California we find the San Andreas fault—that is, the "St. Andrew's fault." Many terrible earthquakes have been caused by the San Andreas fault, but you can't see it. It does its work underground. It's not visible, but when it does its work, everybody knows it by all the shaking that goes on. It's the same way with Andrew himself. In his own way he shook up this world, but he worked underground. Undercover. A quieter disciple than the rest.

That's significant. Not everything can be calculated by numbers. Everyone does his or her part. God gives the increase and God gets the glory. So there's a great story here for all of us. We look at the accomplishment of Simon Peter and say, "I could never do that." We look at the deeds of Paul or John and say, "I could never do that." But we all can be an Andrew. Andrew has been so inspiring in that sense that some churches name their calling program, "The Andrew Committee" or "The Andrew Team." We could at least do that. Instead of worrying about millions, we can concern ourselves with the one or two in our own circle who need Jesus. You can be an Andrew for them.

*Flash*Points

1. Why is it important for every Christian to know how to take a back seat?

2. In what ways can Christians work "undercover"?

Another landmark that's named for Andrew is the Cross of St. Andrew. According to legend, Andrew ministered near the Black Sea in present-day Russia, though others say he worked in Scotland. As a result, Scotland adopted Andrew as their patron saint. From tradition, we also know that Andrew died a martyr's death. He had evidently converted the wife of a prominent military governor. The governor had Andrew executed on a cross shaped liked an "X." That X-shaped cross came to be known as the Cross of St. Andrew.

You have seen the Cross of St. Andrew, but you may not realize it. It appears on the British flag, the "Union Jack," as a white "X" along with two other crosses. Isn't it fitting that Andrew, who wasn't afraid to be in the background, shares that famous flag with two other people who weren't even apostles—St. George and St. Patrick? I don't think he cares much.

It was once said that the sun never set on the Union Jack. The British Empire has gradually gotten smaller so we can no longer say that. But in another kingdom, the influence of Andrew still lives. His influence unfurls as a banner in the kingdom of God because he was willing to bring one, who brought another, who brought another. He is an example for all of us. One simple person can win the lost. Because of that principle, the sun never sets on the kingdom of Heaven.

Andrew's banner stills waves. The question is, will we pick it up and carry it into a new millennium? If Andrew were here today, I think he would encourage us to do it. He might say, "I know you can do it. If I can, anybody can."

Four
Drawn to the Light

If you shine a light, something will be drawn to it. For example, if you shine a light in your backyard in the summer, many things will be attracted to it. All kinds of things. Strange things.

Jesus is the light of the world and He attracts crowds. All kinds of people. Different and strange people. Sometimes this fact is stated as a criticism of the church. People ridicule the strange people who come to Christ and to the church. (Not in your church or mine, mind you. We're all OK!) When you think about it, it would be surprising if Jesus, the light of the world, did not attract all kinds of people. They need Him and need to hear what the gospel teaches. Consider this different, even humorous, incident in the life of Jesus as people were drawn to Him.

> A few days later, when Jesus again entered Capernaum, the people heard that he had come home. So many gathered that there was no room left, not even outside the door, and he preached the word to them. Some men came, bringing to him a paralytic, carried by four of them. Since they could not get him to Jesus because of the crowd, they made an opening in the roof above Jesus and, after digging through it, lowered the mat the paralyzed man was lying on. When Jesus saw their faith, he said to the paralytic, "Son, your sins are forgiven."
>
> Now some teachers of the law were sitting there, thinking to themselves, "Why does this follow talk like that? He's

blaspheming! Who can forgive sins but God alone?"
   Immediately Jesus knew in his spirit that this was what
they were thinking in their hearts, and he said to them,
"Why are you thinking these things? Which is easier: to say
to the paralytic, 'Your sins are forgiven,' or to say, 'Get up,
take your mat and walk'? But that you may know that the
Son of Man has authority on earth to forgive sins . . . ." He
said to the paralytic, "I tell you, get up, take your mat and
go home." He got up, took his mat and walked out in full
view of them all. This amazed everyone and they praised
God, saying, "We have never seen anything like this!"

Mark 2:1-12

Jesus had come home to Capernaum and a lot of people
had been drawn to His light. They may have been in Simon
Peter's house since this was where Jesus stayed when He
was in Capernaum and was His base of operation. Many
people came, not just to see Him heal, but also to hear Him
preach. We modern day preachers have to work all week to
get a crowd up for Sunday, but just a rumor of Jesus preaching brought great crowds. They jammed inside the house and
outside the house, listening from the windows and blocking
the doors.

There were several men that day, at least five, who were
desperate to come to Jesus—a paralytic and the four men
carrying him. Many other men may have been with the paralytic, but we especially notice the four who carried him.
When they got to the place where Jesus was preaching, they
were faced with a great problem. How were they going to
get through this crowd? These men were drawn to the light,
but how were they going to get there?

In the Middle East in those days, many of the roofs were
flat, made of thatched mud. The houses were built with outside stairs leading up to the roof. It would be fairly easy to
reach the roof and break through. These men knew this and
would not be deterred. They came straight through to Jesus.

I imagine it was a humorous scene to watch them break
through the roof. Imagine this scene: Jesus is preaching and

He hears a noise over His head. He keeps on preaching. Then there's more noise, then dust and thatch from the roof begin to fall—getting in people's eyes and in their beards. Then there's a shaft of light. And then down comes this man lowered on a pallet. It's interesting that Jesus was absolutely delighted with this, but then Jesus always rejoiced in seeing great faith. The friends of the paralytic had faith—a special faith, a dramatic faith, a dynamic faith. You and I can have this faith if we are willing to learn from them.

*Flash*Points

1. When have you been listening to someone speak or teach when some unusual event has occurred?

2. How might speakers or teachers respond differently to an interruption than Jesus did to this one?

A Faith Accompanied by Compassion

These five men exhibited the kind of faith we need to have. Their faith, first of all, was accompanied by compassion. You might think that faith would automatically bring forth compassion. Not always. If faith is given free reign, it will bring forth compassion. But all of us have met people who know book, chapter, and verse of Scripture, yet have little compassion in their hearts. They can quote Scripture freely, but they do not live it. These men, however, had a faith that allowed them to look at a man's need and try to meet that need. They didn't see his need as some vague thing.   •

We can look at statistics on how many people in the world are starving, but that probably doesn't reach us. If we see a television special produced by folk such as World Vision and see just one face of one person who's starving, that may move us. These men were captivated the same way—willing to pay particular attention to a particular friend in his particular need. That's not always easy. It's usually easier to ignore the need.

Julia Ward Howe, who composed "The Battle Hymn of the Republic," once asked Charles Sumner, a well-known senator, to help a person in serious need. He told her, "I've gotten so busy, I just can't pay attention to individuals." She replied, "That's remarkable. Even God himself has not reached that stage yet."

She was right. Our God is concerned about individuals, and He wants us to be concerned about individuals. But sometimes there's not much passion in our compassion. We have good wishes for people. We don't wish anybody ill, but we don't have that passionate compassion.

A marriage counselor was working with a couple. As they talked, he became more and more convinced that all that was really needed was for the husband to show more affection to his wife. The counselor tried to explain this to the husband, but he wasn't getting through. Finally, he did something no counselor should ever do. On impulse, he went over to the wife, hugged her and kissed her and then looked at the husband and said, "Now that's what she needs, and she needs it every day."

The husband scratched his head and said, "Well, OK. But it's going be hard to get here on Thursdays. That's our bowling night."

*Flash*Points

1. When were you most recently moved to do something out of compassion?

2. Compassion is essentially love. How are faith and love related?

3. In what settings is it difficult to care about individuals?

A Faith Expressed by Action

A strong faith also demands that we take personal responsibility and act. The four men in this Scripture passage had a dynamic faith that was not only accompanied by compassion, but also was expressed by action. These men lived out what James taught: "Faith without works is dead" (James 2:20, KJV). Not, "faith without works feels bad," or, "faith without works is sick," but, "faith without works is dead." These men understood the truth that faith has to have legs on it. Faith is a muscular word. Faith is something that demands action on our part. We have often tried to divorce these two concepts: grace versus works; faith versus deeds. We say we're saved by grace and not by works, so we leave works completely out. Or we talk about our responsibilities and forget grace.

The fact is you can't separate these two things. You may discuss them separately, but in practical terms of how life is lived, faith and deeds must come together. Our deeds reveal our creeds. We don't want to be like the Pharisees, who were concerned with their ritualistic deeds. Notice that Jesus never condemned the Pharisees for their deeds in and of themselves. He condemned them for their wrong priorities and wrong motivations. In fact, Jesus commended the Pharisees for their deeds. We, then, need to have deeds that are consistent with our faith.

Besides, what else is anybody going to see except our deeds? Someone may claim to have faith, but we can't see his heart. All we can see is how that faith is translated into action. We don't have to become hypocritical like the Pharisees, but we can match devotion of the heart with the deeds that follow; the fruit that is born from our faith.

In Jimmy Carter's best-selling book, *Living Faith,* Carter talks about how faith affects every aspect of his life. He originally wanted to call that book, *Faith Is a Verb,* but his publishers instead opted for *Living Faith.* Both titles work because a living faith is a faith that finds expression in action. That's what makes the faith alive.

Let's look at a few analogies that show how faith and works are in dynamic tension. Can we separate the brain from the spinal column? Technically, yes, we can. You can dissect a body and separate the parts and say, "This is the brain," and "That is the spinal column." But do we want them separated in the physical life we live? No, we want them to stay connected so we can function. The brain needs to send and receive the messages necessary to operate our body. In practical terms, they cannot be separated and still fulfill their function.

Can we separate the heart from the blood vessels? Sure. There's the heart and there are the blood vessels. But in practical terms we don't want them separated because the blood needs to be pumped from the heart through those vessels to do its work.

In the same way, faith needs deeds. Let's suppose somebody claimed to be the greatest baseball fan of all times. We might ask him, "What makes you the biggest fan ever? Do you know more about the game than anyone else? Have you, for instance, memorized all the stats?"

"Nope, they're not important."

"Do you have a favorite team?" we might ask.

"Yeah."

"Is it in the American or National League?"

"Oh, there are leagues?" asks the supposed greatest baseball fan of all time.

"Yeah, there are leagues," we reply.

The more we discuss it, the more we realize this guy who claims to be the greatest baseball fan of all times doesn't know a thing about baseball. He has done nothing that shows he's a fan. He may indeed be a great baseball fan, but all the evidence is stacked against him.

Or let's say somebody claims to be the greatest romantic of all times.

"When was the last time you took your wife out for dinner?" you ask.

"Let's see," he says. "I can't rightly remember. It was a few years ago. I took her out for a burger somewhere."

"What did you get your wife for your anniversary?" we ask.

"Anniversary," he says. "I've got one of those, but I don't rightly remember when it is."

He may claim to be the greatest romantic of all times, but the evidence indicates otherwise. We need to understand that the only thing people can see is the way faith works in our life. These four men and their paralytic friend understood that. They had a faith that was accompanied by action.

*Flash*Points

1. When have you ever felt miserable because you wanted to help someone but couldn't? Describe how that felt.

2. How does love for God inspire you to show love for others?

3. Why does a person with faith want to do good works?

Faith Undaunted by Obstacles

The paralytic and his friends had a faith undaunted by
obstacles. There will always be obstacles in life. Everyone
of us will experience things that strive to weaken our faith or
to discourage it.

These men faced several obstacles. First, there was the
obstacle of their own personal convenience. It's just not convenient to take a paralyzed man with you anywhere. It
would have been a lot faster if they could have just gone to
hear Jesus without this paralyzed friend. It's not convenient
to carry a person around. It put a strain on their energy and
their muscles.

Then there was the crowd blocking the doorway and access
to the roof. But nothing stopped them. They broke all the
way through. All along the way, they may have asked questions—the questions any of us ask when we're trying to live
out our faith. Is this really worth it? Do we look foolish?
What will this cost?

Part of what helps us overcome obstacles is the blessing of
friendship. Not everyone has friends like this paralyzed man.
For example, another paralyzed man in the Bible sat by the
pool of Bethesda every day for thirty-eight years. When
Jesus met the man and asked him if he wanted to get well,
he replied, "I have no one to help me into the pool when the
water is stirred. While I am trying to get in, someone else
goes down ahead of me" (John 5:7). But the man in this passage had several friends who were willing to help him.

. These men helping their friend create a picture of what the
church ought to be about—lifting up those who are hurting
and bringing them to Jesus. All of us at one time or another
find ourselves in need of that kind of ministry. It's interesting that Jesus "saw their faith" (Mark 2:5). That goes back
to faith in action. Jesus saw their faith. It wasn't just the
faith of the four friends, but also the faith of the paralyzed
man. He wanted to meet Jesus more than anybody. But his
faith was strengthened by his friends. As we share our own

faith with each other and minister to each other, our faith is strengthened by the community of believers. Jesus was delighted to see it.

*Flash*Points

1. When have you allowed questions and doubts (which are normal) to become an obstacle to doing something good?

2. When have friends helped you overcome an obstacle?

3. In what situation do you currently need some help from friends?

4. Who is a friend you need to help more in overcoming obstacles?

Faith Rewarded by Mercy

The man came to be healed of paralysis, but Jesus said, "Son, your sins are forgiven" (Mark 2:5). Some have wondered if Jesus said this because this man's illness was the result of a sin. Perhaps he sinned and harmed his body in some way to cause the paralysis. Or perhaps he was being punished for some kind of unforgiven sin. All that is mere speculation. There is no indication of that in the text. The one thing we can say for sure is that, by addressing the man's sin condition, Jesus was saying, "You've got a bigger problem than your paralysis. You've got a sin problem. I'm going to take care of that."

Suppose you were to ask a paralyzed person, "Would you rather be healed so you can walk, or be forgiven so you have an eternity forever with the Lord?" What do you think his or her answer would be? What's interesting is this man received both—forgiveness of sins and physical healing. Why is that? Why did Jesus grant both of these things to him, but not to others? I can't answer that. But I can tell you this: Every sick person will someday be healed. Some will be healed in Heaven and some will be healed here. What we see now are little glimmers of the healing power that will be demonstrated fully in eternity. Everyone will be healed.

God shows us some of that healing here so we'll know what to expect in Heaven. I've prayed for people who have gotten well and for people who haven't gotten well. I prayed earnestly in every case, and I can't explain why some were healed and some were not. But I do know that in every case, if a person genuinely asks for forgiveness, they can be assured that they've received it. In the same manner, we can be assured of ultimate healing in Heaven. Forgiveness is the most important thing. That's why Jesus addressed it here.

These men got all the way through to Jesus. Doubt looks for excuses; faith finds a way. Author David Redding said, "Miracles don't happen on the breath of faith. Miracles happen when faith has found its second wind." And so this man received not only the healing of the body, but the healing of the soul.

Not everyone was happy about Jesus' forgiving of sins, especially the teachers of the law. They said, "Why does this fellow talk like that? He's blaspheming! Who can forgive sins but God alone?" (Mark 2:7). On a certain level, their response was understandable. Forgiveness of sins *is* God's area of responsibility. But Jesus is the Son of God. So Jesus posed an interesting question. He asked them whether it was easier to say the man's sins were forgiven or to heal him.

There are two answers to that question. The first answer is that they were both equally easy for Jesus. But from a human perspective, one seems easier than the other. It's easier to say, "Your sins are forgiven," because nobody can prove whether it happened or not. No one can discern what is in another's heart. But if you say, "Rise and walk," and the person cannot, then you are shown to be a charlatan or a fake. So Jesus decided to show them the seemingly harder thing. He said, "Get up, take your mat and go home" (Mark 2:11). The man got up in full view of them all. Jesus' outward healing ability proved His inward divine identity, and demonstrated His power to forgive sins.

Everyone was amazed and said, "We have never seen anything like this!" (Mark 2:12). The man got much more than what he asked for—not less. Not all of us will face the problem of physical paralysis, but all of us will face a sin problem. God is abundant in mercy. He delights in giving us more than we could ask or imagine. God is not miserly with His grace. If we have the same dynamic faith as the man who was paralyzed and his friends, we too will discover that God does even more than we ask. But we have to have the determination to press through to Jesus, no matter what. This is the tough muscular faith the Bible describes. We need this dynamic biblical faith if we want to be healed.

*Flash*Points

1. If you were face to face with Jesus and He said, "Your sins are forgiven," what would that mean to you?

2. What sorts of healing do you look forward to in eternity?

3. In what situation do you need to be reassured that God is generous with grace?

Gene Appel, in his book, *Dream Intruders,* tells a story about Lloyd Ogilvie, former chaplain of the United States Senate, and previous minister of the Hollywood Presbyterian Church. Ogilvie, deeply proud of his Scottish heritage, planned a vacation to the Highlands of Scotland where he could enjoy the culture and the land and get in touch with his roots. Every day he hiked and thought and prayed. One day he went out without telling anyone where he was going. He slipped on a rock, fell into a gorge and lost consciousness. The fall broke his leg in several places and tore some ligaments.

When he awoke, he began to worry, *They won't find me down here. Nobody knows where I am. It may be a long time before they even miss me.* It gets pretty cold in the Scottish highlands at night. Ogilvie began to fear that he might freeze to death. So he determined that he would try to get back to the main road. He couldn't walk, but he got up on his hands and knees and crawled. As he got about halfway to the road, he began to despair of ever getting home. He also got a little lightheaded and began to think, *Maybe it's just best if I give up.* That's when he was encouraged by a Scripture text that came to his mind:

> "For I know the plans I have for you," declares the Lord, "plans to prosper you and not to harm you, plans to give you hope and a future. Then you will call upon me and come and pray to me, and I will listen to you. You will seek me and find me when you seek me with all your heart. I will be found by you," declares the Lord, "and will bring you back from captivity."
>
> Jeremiah 29:11-14

Ogilvie had the courage to press on because of that great promise. No matter what happened, there was a future for him. Eventually he made it to the road, was found, and was taken to the hospital where he recovered. His determination was the same determination these five men had when they pressed through to Jesus regardless of the obstacles. It's that kind of faith our Lord delights in rewarding.

*Flash*Points

1. Look at the quotation above (Jeremiah 29:11-14). Circle the words or phrases that are most meaningful to you.

2. In what way is God currently urging you to press forward?

If you have this determined kind of faith, then you too will receive the reward of His abundant mercy—greater blessings than you ever could have imagined. No matter how things look on earth, beautiful mercies from Heaven will flow to you from a God who delights to give them to you. It may be something wonderful and special will happen in your life and people will say today, as they said one day in Capernaum, "We have never seen anything like this."

Five
I Saw the Light

Imagine for a moment what it would be like to have been born blind. What would it be like never to have seen your mother's face—or your own? Never to have seen the beautiful colors of a sunset or a rainbow? That's hard to imagine, since we can't forget what we already have seen. John tells us about just such a man in chapter 9, verses 1-11.

As he went along, he saw a man blind from birth. His disciples asked him, "Rabbi, who sinned, this man or his parents, that he was born blind?"

"Neither this man nor his parents sinned," said Jesus, "but this happened so that the work of God might be displayed in his life. As long as it is day, we must do the work of him who sent me. Night is coming, when no one can work. While I am in the world, I am the light of the world."

Having said this, he spit on the ground, made some mud with the saliva, and put it on the man's eyes. "Go," he told him, "wash in the Pool of Siloam" (this word means Sent). So the man went and washed, and came home seeing.

His neighbors and those who had formerly seen him begging asked, "Isn't this the same man who used to sit and beg?" Some claimed that he was. Others said, "No, he only looks like him."

But he himself insisted, "I am the man."

"How then were your eyes opened?" they demanded.

He replied, "The man they call Jesus made some mud and put it on my eyes. He told me to go to Siloam and wash. So I went and washed, and then I could see."

The Gospels feature many people who were blind and then healed by Christ, but this is the only case we know of in which the person was born blind.

Imagine what it would be like to be healed of blindness. Do you suppose the man didn't even want to blink for fear of missing something? Do you think maybe he didn't want to go to sleep that night because he wanted to keep looking at things? I imagine he saw great beauty in things we take for granted. And when he did go to sleep, perhaps he dreamed in colors and shapes for the first time in his life.

The Gospel of John records the miracles—the signs that Jesus gave to prove His authority and power. John then compares these physical acts to spiritual truths. As Jesus opened blind eyes, so He opens the eyes of the heart and gives us spiritual insight. As Jesus brought light into this blind man's life, He proclaimed that He was the light of the world (John 9:5). We do no violence to this text when we say that this miracle helps us see the light about several important truths.

*Flash*Points

1. If you were the congenitally blind person who was healed, how would you have felt at the end of the passage quoted above?

2. In what area do you need spiritual insight?

3. In what area do you need the eyes of your heart opened?

Seeing the Light About Sin and Sickness

The disciples made this blind man the subject of their debate, while Jesus saw him as the subject of compassion. As David Redding says, "The disciples were philosophizing when they should have been philanthropizing." They wanted to bring up the debate that goes all the way back to the book of Job. The disciples said, "Who sinned, this man or his parents, that he was born blind?" They already made the assumption that somebody sinned. I suppose their position was that this man's parents sinned, and so God punished them by afflicting their child with blindness.

What did they mean by asking, "Was he born blind because he sinned?" Did they believe in reincarnation? No, but some did believe that it was possible to have prenatal sin, meaning that you could sin while you were in the womb. I don't know what a baby in the womb can do to sin, but some believed it was possible.

Jesus didn't get involved in their debate. In fact, He told them this wasn't the issue at all. The issue was that God wanted to bring glory into this man's life. God wanted to take the man's life and do something wonderful with it. That can happen whether we are healed physically or not. I can guarantee that whenever you face a trial or sickness, God is willing to make something glorious out of it.

But does sin lead to sickness? All sin leads to some kind of suffering. The truth is that we are not so much punished *for* our sins, but we are punished *by* our sins. It is true that sin will eventually lead to some kind of suffering, but it is

not true that all suffering began with individual sin. There
are occasions in the Bible where God punished people with
some kind of sickness, but that is rare. It is certainly rare
enough that we ought not think that every time we're sick it
is because we have done something wrong. Rarely does a
specific sin result in a specific suffering or illness.

We live in an imperfect world because of our rebellion
against God. Every aspect of our life is flawed. Our spiritual
life is flawed and our physical life is flawed. What frustrates
many of us is how close to perfect this life is. The life many
of us experience is a beautiful life punctuated by occasional
tragedy—not a tragic life punctuated by occasional beauty.
This earth produces what we need for food as well as just
enough sunshine and rain. Seed time and harvest are con-
stant while drought and flood and tornado are occasional.
Most of the time nature works to our advantage.

The same is true with our bodies. Most of the time we
fight off the germs and the viruses, but there are times we
don't. On one occasion Jesus was asked about this controversy. He talked about a recent event, saying, "Those eighteen
who died when the tower in Siloam fell on them—do you
think they were more guilty than all the others living in
Jerusalem?" (Luke 13:4). Jesus was basically saying that
we're all in trouble! We all sin enough that if God were
going to punish our sin with sickness, we'd be sick all the
time. It isn't wise to consider sickness the direct result of sin.

But God can provide healing for the body or spirit in such
a way that whatever illness you're going through can be
redeemed. Some people don't receive healing of the body,
but God gives them special grace to overcome.

A friend of mine shared this story with me. A member of
the Blind Golfer's Association was introduced to Arnold
Palmer. Palmer asked, "How in the world do you play golf?"

The blind golfer said, "My caddie goes to the hole and rings
a bell, and I try to hit the ball toward the sound of the bell."

"Well, that's amazing," said Arnold Palmer. "Are you pretty good?"

He said, "Oh, I'm good. I'm good enough to challenge you to a round of golf."

"Wow!" said Palmer. "I'll take you up on that. When do you want to meet?"

"How about 10:30 tonight?" the blind man replied.

That story sounds suspiciously fictional, but there are plenty of real people who learn how to redeem their disability. I'll tell you a story that I know is true. In our hymn book are many songs written by Fanny Crosby. She was afflicted with blindness when she was approximately eight. A medical treatment went wrong and caused her blindness. Rather than giving in to bitterness and despair, she looked at it as a blessing. It helped her shut out certain parts of the world and concentrate on the poetry in her soul. She was convinced that some of her great poetry would not have come to her if she'd been distracted by sight. It's interesting that in the first year of her blindness, just as a young girl, she wrote this little verse,

> Oh, what a happy child am I, although I cannot see!
> I am resolved that in this world contented I will be.
> How many blessings I enjoy that other people don't.
> To weep and sigh because I'm blind, I cannot, and I won't.

It is a great thing when blind eyes are healed, but it's an even greater thing when spirits are strengthened and lifted like Fanny Crosby's.

*Flash*Points

1. In what situations that call for compassion do you find yourself philosophizing instead of philanthropizing?

2. How has God taken things such as sickness and used them to bring glory into your life in some way?

3. How does a wise understanding that we're all flawed and we're all in trouble keep us from entertaining self-pity?

Seeing the Light of Hypocrisy and Legalism

The healing of the man born blind helps to shed some light on sin and sickness, but it also helps us see the light about hypocrisy and legalism. When this man was healed, you would have expected everyone to be happy about it. Not the Pharisees! Unfortunately their hypocrisy and legalism gave them very little joy in life.

> They brought to the Pharisees the man who had been blind. Now the day on which Jesus had made the mud and opened the man's eyes was a Sabbath. Therefore the Pharisees also asked him how he had received his sight. "He put mud on my eyes," the man replied, "and I washed, and now I see."
>
> Some of the Pharisees said, "This man is not from God, for he does not keep the Sabbath."
>
> But others asked, "How can a sinner do such miraculous signs?" So they were divided.
>
> John 9:13-16

Why were the Pharisees upset? Because they believed Jesus had broken the law. The law said, "Remember the Sabbath day by keeping it holy" (Exodus 20:8). One of the ways the Jews obeyed this law was by not working. However, the Pharisees and the scribes were the ones who decided what was work and what wasn't. In their minds, they saw three ways in which Jesus had broken the Sabbath Law.

First, He used saliva to make mud. The Pharisees had decided that if you had to spit on the Sabbath, you had to spit on a rock so wouldn't make mud. Making mud was work. Jesus spit in the dirt and made mud to put on the man's eyes.

The act of using the saliva was work also. This seems very unhygienic to us, but even today there are some who think saliva has medicinal qualities. Even more so in Jesus day, the saliva of a holy man was thought to have medicinal qual-ities. To the Pharisees, saliva was a medicine and they didn't believe you should be medicating on the Sabbath. You could keep people from dying on the Sabbath, but you couldn't try to make them well. So when Jesus applied saliva, that too was considered a violation of the law.

The biggest problem was that the man got well. That was a violation of the law because, to the legalists, healing some-one was definitely work!

The Pharisees indicted Jesus with three violations of the law as they interpreted it. There was very little joy in these people, and very little opportunity to rejoice. They called the man in and tried to make him answer for the healing. What had he done? Nothing. But hypocrites have little compas-sion, and these men needed to direct their anger at someone. First they assaulted the man, and then his parents.

"What have you to say about him? It was your eyes he opened."

The man replied, "He is a prophet."

The Jews still did not believe that he had been blind and had received his sight until they sent for the man's parents.

"Is this your son?" they asked. "Is this the one you say was born blind? How is it that now he can see?"

And of course the man's parents were afraid of the outcome, so they said:

"We don't know. Ask him. He is of age; he will speak for himself."

The Pharisees brought the man back and put him under oath.

"Give glory to God," they said. "We know this man is a sinner."
He replied, "Whether he is a sinner or not, I don't know. One thing I do know. I was blind but now I see!"

John 9:17-25

I love this man's sense of humor! It's as if he said, "Funny you can't figure out who this man is—even a man as ignorant as I knows that it takes a special man to heal blindness!"

Then they asked him, "What did he do to you? How did he open your eyes?"
He answered, "I have told you already and you did not listen. Why do you want to hear it again? Do you want to become his disciples, too?"   John 9:26, 27

What a great answer!

Then they hurled insults at him and said, "You are this fellow's disciple! We are disciples of Moses! We know that God spoke to Moses, but as for this fellow, we don't even know where he comes from."   John 9:28, 29

It's interesting that the Pharisees were willing to accept by faith that God spoke to Moses, but they were not willing to accept by faith anything about Jesus. Once again the man demonstrated his wit and intelligence with his answer.

"Now that is remarkable! You don't know where he comes from, yet he opened my eyes. We know that God does not listen to sinners. He listens to the godly man who does his will. Nobody has ever heard of opening the eyes of a man born blind. If this man were not from God, he could do nothing."

To this they replied, "You were steeped in sin at birth; how dare you lecture us!" And they threw him out.

John 9:30-34

When Scripture says they threw the man out, that means they put him out of the synagogue. He was no longer able to come to the temple or the synagogue to worship. But what had this man done wrong? Nothing. Because of their anger at Jesus, the Pharisees put this man out. Hypocrisy and legalism leave little room for joy or compassion, and even less for objectivity. A healthy skepticism is good, but that is different from bull-headedness. Alger Fitch summarized these events in this manner:

• Jesus saw the blind man and said, "I see a need and I will meet it."

• The disciples said, "I see a problem and I'll raise it."

• The blind man said, "I see an opportunity and I'll accept it."

• The Pharisees said, "I see a sign and I'll reject it."

*Flash*Points

1. Try to detect where hypocrisy and legalism might be creeping up on you by asking yourself this question: "Where in my life is there little joy, little compassion, and little objectivity?"

2. Which of the four responses to this incident listed above in bullets describes your participation in your local congregation?

The Pharisees rejected Jesus even though they saw Him do things they had never seen before. They weren't willing to examine the claims of Christ. Sometimes we use the word "see" to represent finding insight. We may talk about people with insight and say they can see better than we can. Or when we face a problem in school and finally understand the answer we might say, "Oh, I see!" Or someone struggles to explain something to us until we finally understand and say, "Oh, I see."

The Pharisees thought they could see, but could they? Who remained blind in this situation? A man who was physically blind was healed. He had been spiritually blind but was enabled to see the truth. Only the blindness of the Pharisees remained.

*Flash*Points

1. What do you think sharpens spiritual sight?

2. How can you find out whether you're spiritually blind in some area?

Seeing the Light About Jesus and Grace

This miracle sheds light for us on sin and sickness, hypocrisy and legalism, and it also helps us to see the light about Jesus and grace.

Think about how Jesus healed this man using common elements. What's more common than saliva and dirt? Many people have wondered why Jesus did it this way. He healed in many different ways; Jesus could heal even when He wasn't present. So why in this case did He choose saliva and dirt? Perhaps there is a spiritual message in the elements. Clay often represents flawed humanity. We know from Genesis 2:7 and Psalms 103:14 that our bodies are made from dust so perhaps Jesus used the dust from the ground to remind us of our humanity. From the clay that Jesus put on the man's eyes He produced faith and trust in this man.

Have you ever had a speck in your eye? Even a little thing can feel like a boulder. Imagine how it felt to have Jesus rub your eyes with dirt! It may have been uncomfortable. Sometimes before we change, we have to feel some discomfort about our sins. We have to develop some divine dissatisfaction.

Then the man had to wash out the dirt with water in the pool of Siloam (John 9:7), which tells us that we need to be cleansed of our sins. We need to wash away those things that inhibit spiritual sight.

As this man was healed, he saw a lesson about God's grace and His willingness to cleanse us from all iniquity. He also saw something else about Jesus' grace. When this man was rejected by the Pharisees, Jesus sought him out, and when He found him, He said:

> "Do you believe in the Son of Man?"
> "Who is he, sir?" the man asked. "Tell me so that I may believe in him."
> Jesus said, "You have now seen him; in fact, he is the one speaking with you."
> Then the man said, "Lord, I believe," and he worshiped him."
>
> John 9:35-38

At first the man called the healer, "Jesus." Then he called him "a prophet." Finally he called him "Messiah" and "Lord." It's a wonderful thing to see the light of day but a far greater thing to see the light of the world. We may suppose that the man felt better to be kicked out of the synagogue but find Christ than to be in the synagogue and not find Christ.

Whatever crisis you're going through, something will give. Some kind of healing will come. God will work. Not every sick person was healed while Jesus was on earth, but there were moments when Jesus performed beautiful healings with the power of the Father to show us what He wants to do for us spiritually. And yet we are like the Pharisees saying, "Well, we can already see. We're not blind!" To that Jesus replies, "If that's the way it is, then your guilt remains." If the Pharisees had admitted their own blindness, they too could have been healed and been enabled to see.

*Flash*Points

1. When do you think God has used common objects or activities to produce in you faith and trust?

2. Which step of the man's healing is most familiar to your experience?
   __ understanding that you're flawed (dust)
   __ seeing how your flaws hurt when rubbed in
   __ becoming cleansed from flaws (washing in the pool)
   __ being rejected by others but sought out by God
   __ coming to understand Jesus in a greater way—from miracle worker to Lord

Jesus gave this man not only physical sight but spiritual sight. Jesus was not willing for him to have one without having the opportunity for the other. That is the testimony not only of this blind man, but of a man who lived in the 1700s. He was a seaman by trade. Working the sea is a rough life for anyone, but rougher for him because he managed slaving vessels. He lived a life of dissipation as a libertine, exploring every vice known by men of the sea. One day his lifestyle began to disgust him. The slave trade disgusted him. His own habits disgusted him. He found Christ—and was so transformed that he became a minister. His name was John Newton, and you know his testimony for you have sung it many times in the song he wrote:

> Amazing grace, how sweet the sound.
>   That saved a wretch like me.
> I once was lost but now am found,
>   Was blind but now I see.

The *Six* Morning Light

Many people assume there was only one good Samaritan in the Bible, but the passage we want to explore in this chapter points to another. In this incident, one man among a group of ten dared to come back and express his praise to Jesus—and he was a Samaritan. He is also a beautiful example of thankfulness and praise.

> Now on his way to Jerusalem, Jesus traveled along the border between Samaria and Galilee. As he was going into a village, ten men who had leprosy met him. They stood at a distance and called out in a loud voice, "Jesus, Master, have pity on us!"
> When he saw them, he said, "Go, show yourselves to the priests." And as they went, they were cleansed.
> One of them, when he saw he was healed, came back, praising God in a loud voice. He threw himself at Jesus' feet and thanked him—and he was a Samaritan.
> Jesus asked, "Were not all ten cleansed? Where are the other nine? Was no one found to return and give praise to God except this foreigner?" Then he said to him, "Rise and go; your faith has made you well."
>
> Luke 17:11-19

Only Luke, of all the Gospel writers, recorded this story. As a physician, perhaps Luke was more interested in the healing miracles of Jesus. He was also Gentile and therefore interested in how Jesus reached out to Gentiles and other outcasts. This story, then, had several of Luke's favorite themes.

*Flash*Points

1. In this passage, it's the foreigner—the Samaritan—who is the good guy. If this incident were occurring with Jesus on earth today, what "foreigner" might be the one to return?

2. Put yourself in the place of Luke, the doctor. What is most interesting to you about Jesus' method of healing?

They All Had a Problem

Ten were healed and one, a Samaritan, came back to give thanks. At first these men seem much alike. They were alike, for instance, in that they all had the same problem—leprosy. What was it like to be a leper in Jesus' day?

Lepers were shunned by polite society. They had to announce their arrival in any town and their presence to anyone approaching by shouting, "Unclean! Unclean!" People thought leprosy was much more contagious than it really is, which made them afraid to be around those who were stricken. That's why leper colonies were formed.

This ailment, which was common yet frightening in Bible times, was a virtual death sentence, but death came a little bit at a time. Day by day, the person with leprosy lost feeling in his or her extremities and the resulting injuries caused disfiguration little by little. People with leprosy often could not bear to look at their own images. They were separated from family and friends. Their only sense of community was with the other lepers.

What the Bible describes as leprosy is not just Hansen's disease, which is what we call leprosy today. It also included a whole range of skin illnesses that affected people in the Middle East. Because lepers were isolated from others, it caused people to be afraid. In a sense, it was like the AIDS of its day in that people were greatly afraid of it. No one ever dared touch a leper.

Many in the Bible suffered from this kind of skin ailment—some permanently, some temporarily. Among those who suffered from leprosy were Moses, Miriam, Naaman, Uzziah, and the four lepers of Samaria. In the New Testament, there was a man known as Simon the Leper, at whose home Jesus visited and even ate (Matthew 26:6; Mark 14:3). Of course, we know that Jesus healed lepers on more than one occasion. Jesus even dared to touch them (Matthew 8:3; Mark 1:41; Luke 5:12, 13). On the occasion in our study, he healed ten. Ten men living the horrible nightmare of leprosy were each given a new dawn of hope by Jesus—a new morning, a new life.

Even today leprosy fills people with fear and sends chills up the spine. Just recently I read in Jimmy Carter's book, *Living Faith,* about his mother, Miss Lillian, who joined the Peace Corps when she was elderly and went to work among the sick of India. Jimmy Carter wrote a poem about his mother's first encounter with leprosy titled "Miss Lillian Sees Leprosy for the First Time."

When I nursed in a clinic near Bombay,
a small girl, shielding all her leprous sores,
crept inside the door. I moved away,
but then the doctor said, "You take this case!"
First I found a mask and put it on,
quickly gave the child a shot and then,
not well, I slipped away to be alone
and scrubbed my entire body red and raw.
I faced her treatment every week with dread
and loathing for the chore, not the child.
As time passed, I was less afraid
and managed not to turn my face away.
Her spirit bloomed as sores began to fade.
She'd raise her anxious, searching eyes to mine,
to show she trusted me. We'd smile and say a few
Marathi words, then reach and hold
each other's hands. And then love grew between
us, so that when I kissed her lips
I didn't feel unclean.

  Even today, leprosy—and other illnesses and disabilities—
can fill us with fear and revulsion. These reactions can be
countered only by love.

*Flash*Points

1. When have you felt like an outcast?

2. How do you think Jesus might behave toward today's AIDS patients?

3. When, if ever, have you had an experience like Miss Lillian's in which you had a change of heart regarding a person's condition or appearance?

These ten men may have had little in common other than leprosy, but this horrible illness united them. It's interesting to note that shared sorrows or adversities often bring people together. Leslie Flynn, in *The Miracles of Jesus,* tells a story about Father Damien, who ministered to lepers in the late 1800s. For years he would begin his sermons by addressing his congregation as, "Brothers . . ." One day, however, as he was serving dinner, some hot soup fell on his foot—but Father Damien didn't feel it. That Sunday he addressed his congregation as, "Fellow lepers . . ." He had become one with them in their suffering.

All Were Humble

All ten of the lepers were humble. They came to Jesus with a great deal of respect. They kept the appropriate distance. And when they called out to Jesus, they said, "Jesus,

Master, have pity on us." These were not men who came to Jesus accusing, "Why did God put me through this?" They did not come to Jesus with theological questions. Perhaps they had heard of His ability to heal, and they simply came in humility and asked for His help.

You have to admire the optimism of this group of men. Faced with a dismal future, they never stopped hoping that things would get better, and they believed Jesus could help them. Since everyone's faith is on a continuum, some of these men may have had more faith than others, but they all had enough faith to come to Jesus with hope for a better future.

When Jesus told them what to do, they were all obedient. Every single one obeyed. This is significant because Jesus' command, "Go show yourselves to the priests," was a strange thing to ask them to do.

According to the Old Testament law, only a priest could declare a leper to be cleansed because leprosy was considered a spiritual problem as well as a medical problem. Because leprosy made its victims unclean in the eyes of the law, lepers were unable to come into the temple or synagogue to worship. So, although only a priest could declare you free from leprosy, the priest rarely saw a leper or saw leprosy cleansed.

Interestingly, Jesus told them to go *before* they were healed. You would think Jesus would heal them and then say, "Go to the priest." Instead Jesus tried to plant a seed in their heart and their mind by first asking them to go. Our text says, "As they went, they were cleansed" (v. 14).

All Were Happy

Jesus rewarded their obedience. They all received healing. They were, we can assume, all happy with what had happened, but they expressed it in different ways. One expressed it in a way superior to the rest. Yes, Jesus was disappointed that only one came back, but I don't think that we should assume that all these men were ungrateful.

I read about a preacher who, when he first heard this story as a child, thought these men were leopards, not lepers. Then, he said, "I got a little bit smarter and I began to think they were leapers." No doubt, they all became leapers when they were healed, but only one came back.

*Flash*Points

1. How did the lepers show their respect to Jesus?

2. Why was Jesus' command to show themselves to the priests so unusual?

3. In what situation have you obeyed God (or not obeyed) even though you were thinking, But I'm not . . . as some of the lepers probably thought?

One Gave Thanks

Why didn't the nine come back? Sometimes I think we are a little bit too hard on the nine. I've heard Thanksgiving sermons in which preachers thundered, "Where were the nine? Where were the nine?" as though they were ungrateful people. Let's speculate on some reasons why the nine did not return.

Maybe they were not expressive. Maybe these nine weren't demonstrative or inclined to talk about their feelings. This brings to mind a lyric that Oscar Hammerstein wrote for the Broadway production of "The Sound of Music." "A bell is no bell 'til you ring it. / A song is no song 'til you sing it. / And love in your heart wasn't put there to stay; / love isn't love 'til you give it away." The same may be said of gratitude. It's one thing to feel it, but it's not true gratitude until it's been given away.

Maybe some of these men were too late in returning. Perhaps others wanted to express gratitude, but they were simply procrastinators. They thought, *I'll go to the priest, then I'll go home, and then I'll try to find Jesus and thank Him.* We can understand that. Many of us live by the credo, "Why do today what you can put off until tomorrow?" So maybe it was a simple lack of discipline for some.

Maybe some were forgetful in the joy of the moment. They were full of joy and eager to see their families. They got caught up in the excitement of being healed and just failed to go back.

Maybe some were in a hurry to put the past behind them—they wanted never to think of leprosy again. That's frequently true with people who have been through traumas in their lives. A lot of them say they never want to talk about the experience. So years later when they finally open up, they know it happened to them, but it's almost as though it happened in a dream, or as if it happened to somebody else. We tend to put things in the past, leave them there, and not deal with them again. Maybe some of these men avoided going back to Jesus in their haste to leave their dreadful past.

Maybe some were arrogant. To be realistic, we should assume that at least one of them was prideful or insensitive. Maybe he thought, *It's about time I got healed! I don't know why I had this problem in the first place. I'm going to go home and celebrate.* Others may have thought that they somehow had accomplished it themselves, thinking, *Hey, I went and found a cure. Look at me. Look what I've accomplished.*

For one reason or another, only one man gave thanks. And look how expressive that one Samaritan was! He came back, "praising God in a loud voice." He threw himself at Jesus' feet and thanked Him. That's enthusiasm! And then Luke says, "He was a Samaritan" (v. 16). Think about that for a moment. Normally Samaritans and Jews wouldn't be together. Jews didn't even eat from the same dishes used by Samaritans. They typically hated each other. The other men probably allowed this Samaritan in their group only because he was a fellow leper. If they were all unclean anyway, they might as well be together. Every organization has its pecking order, and don't you imagine that in this group of ten lepers, the Samaritan was at the low end of the pecking order? And yet, he was the one who came back.

*Flash*Points

1. Which of these reasons for not thanking people are most likely to be yours as well:
   ___ I'm not expressive
   ___ I'm eager to put the past behind me
   ___ I procrastinate until it's too late
   ___ I'm insensitive
   ___ I'm forgetful in the joy of the moment
   ___ I think I deserve the good things

2. Which of the reasons above characterized your earlier life before you grew in your capacity for gratefulness?

3. When, if ever, do you recall thanking someone with the exuberance the Samaritan leper showed?

What Will We Do?

Every day we see signs that people aren't very grateful. A man who worked in a post office handling letters to Santa Claus noticed one year that after Christmas was over and the new year had begun, another letter came for Santa Claus. He thought maybe the child had gotten confused or something, so he opened it and found a thank-you note to Santa Claus for all he'd brought. The worker said that in his years at the post office, thousands of letters had come asking for things, but only this once did he see a letter of thanks to Santa Claus.

In the same way, there are times that we don't thank God. Maybe we are going through tough times, and thankfulness doesn't seem appropriate. I can't tell you why the righteous suffer or why people have to face problems. But if we are going to blame God for every single bad thing that happens, it's only fair that we thank Him for every single good thing that happens. If you do that, you'll find you have a lot more to be thankful for than you thought.

In a sermon preached at Emmanuel Presbyterian Church in Los Angeles, Gary Wilburn told this story: "In 1636 amid the darkness of the Thirty Years War, a German pastor, Martin Rinkard, is said to have buried five thousand of his parishioners in one year. He held an average of fifteen funerals a day. His parish was ravaged by war, death, and economic disaster. In the heart of that darkness, with the cries of fear outside his window, he sat down and wrote a table grace for his children. It has been translated into English and has become a part of many hymn books. This is what Rinkard wrote:

> Now thank we all our God with heart and hands and voices,
> Who wondrous things hath done in whom his world rejoices;
> Who, from our mother's arms, hath blessed us on our way,
> With countless gifts of love, and still is ours today.

Can you muster that same determination to find something good even in the worst of circumstances?

I read an old story many years ago about Matthew Henry. The Bible commentator was once robbed by highwaymen. He decided to go back to his room and find something he could be grateful for. He started a list with, "I thank You that, though I was robbed, I was not killed." He continued, "And I thank You that, while I was injured, I was not injured greatly. I thank You that, while I was robbed of everything I had, I didn't have much on me." Finally, at the bottom of the list, he wrote, "I thank You that I was the one robbed, not the one doing the robbing."

*Flash*Points

1. In light of this sentence, "If we are going to blame God for every single bad thing that happens, it's only fair that we thank him for every single good thing that happens," what would you like to thank God for that's occurred since you got up this morning?

2. How do you suppose the German pastor Martin Rinkard managed to be thankful in the midst of so many deaths?

3. Matthew Henry's sentence, "I thank you that I was the one robbed, not the one doing the robbing" shows a gratefulness for how God had worked in his life. For what work of God in your life are you thankful?

It isn't that rare for only one person out of ten to be thankful. Sometimes the odds are worse. During the worst part of the Civil War, this truth was brought home to Abraham Lincoln. It was customary in those days for the President to see ordinary citizens who dropped by the White House to discuss their causes and concerns. On this day when a woman came to see him, President Lincoln said, "'How can I be of service to you, Madam?"

The lady answered, "Mr. President, I know you are a very busy man. I've not come to ask you for anything. I simply came to bring you this box of cookies."

There was a long silence as tears overflowed the President's eyes. He said to her, "Madam, I am greatly moved by what you have done. Since I have become President, people have come into this office one after another asking for favors and demanding things from me. You are the first person who's ever entered these premises asking no favor, but bringing a gift. I thank you from the bottom of my heart."

Find some way to say "thank you" to somebody who needs to hear it, but certainly to God. Mother Teresa told this story at the National Prayer Breakfast in 1994.

> One evening we went out and picked up four people from the street. One of them was in a most terrible condition. I told the sisters, "You take care of the other three, I'll take care of the one who looks worse." So I did for her all that love could do. I put her in bed. And there was such a beautiful smile on her face. She took hold of my hand and she said two words only, "Thank you." And then she died. I could not help but examine my conscience before her. And I asked, "What would I say if I were in her place?" And my answer was very simple. I would have tried to draw attention to myself. I would have said, "I'm hungry, I'm dying, I'm in pain," or something. But she gave me much more. She gave me her grateful love, and she died with a smile on her face.

To say the words, "thank you," is a small thing, but to hear them is a big thing. Think of a time in your life when someone thanked you. Think of how their gratitude filled you with joy. Remembering how we felt can motivate us to say "thank you" more often to those who deserve to hear it.

*Flash*Points

1. Whom do you know who, like President Lincoln, hears only complaints, not thanks? How could you thank that person?

2. What would have to be in your heart if your last words were to be, "Thank you"?

Thanking God

Of course, we cannot list all the things for which to thank God. While a majority of us will never have to face leprosy, we all have to face sin. Sin, like leprosy, is insidious and dehumanizes us. It too eats away at us, little by little by little. And so we, like this one leper, have much to thank God for. If God had done nothing else for us but save us from our sin, that's plenty to thank Him for.

George McDonald tells of a rabbi who was visited by a

tailor named Mendal. Mendal said to the rabbi, "Doesn't God ever get tired of hearing our praises? When I do my work as a tailor, if someone likes my work and they praise me, I am grateful for their praise. But if they were to come back repeatedly to praise me, it would become an irritation. Doesn't God ever get tired of hearing our praise?"

The rabbi said, "Yes, Mendal, He does. But God knows that we need to praise Him more than He needs to hear the praise. And so God patiently listens to us praise Him."

It's true; there's more benefit for us in praising God than for God in receiving the praise. But the problem with the story is that I'm not sure God has heard so much praise that He gets tired of hearing it. He certainly hasn't heard too much praise from me! I spend little time thanking God compared to asking God for things. So maybe we should try to praise God enough to irritate Him just a little bit—if that would be possible. We praise God because He is worthy of praise and we thank Him because we need to.

*Flash*Points

1. How does it help us to praise God?

2. How does it help us to be thankful to others?

3. What sort of change of heart is wrought by being a thankful person?

All of us are like these ten lepers. All of us have a disease called sin. But anyone who has accepted Christ as Savior and Lord is also like the ten in another way. We have been made pure, or as the Bible said, "whole" (Luke 17:19, KJV). There is really only one question that remains for each of us to ask ourselves: Am I like the one?

Seven

This Little Light of Mine

Not very long ago, Ted Turner made the cover of
Newsweek for a gift of over one billion dollars to United
Nations charities. I don't want to take anything away from
his gift because that was a generous thing for Ted Turner to
do. He could have kept his money. He could have spent it on
himself. He could have wasted it. However, that same week
the news wires also carried a story about a Mississippi
woman who gave $150,000 for scholarship money for poor
students. She had saved this money throughout years of
washing other people's clothes. I believe that woman
deserved to be on the cover of *Newsweek* just as much as
Ted Turner. The poor widow we read about in Luke 21 also
deserves to be on the cover of *Newsweek*.

> As he looked up, Jesus saw the rich putting their gifts into
> the temple treasury. He also saw a poor widow put in two
> very small copper coins. "I tell you the truth," he said, "this
> poor widow has put in more than all the others. All these
> people gave their gifts out of their wealth; but she out of her
> poverty put in all she had to live on." Luke 21:1-4

The offering receptacles in the temple were each marked
with the various places that the money would go. The people
would throw their money into a metal, trumpet-shaped opening and let it rattle around in the bell of that trumpet. The
temple leaders would stand by and watch everything that

went in. What if your church took up the offering that way? Suppose the church decided to put big offering plates in the lobby and you gave your money as you exited while the church leaders watched? I don't think that would go over very well, but that's the way they took up the offering in the temple.

After a long day of discussion and controversy, Jesus deliberately placed himself beside the temple treasury. Why did He do that? In the words of that great baseball player, Yogi Berra, "You can observe a lot just by looking." That's true. That day Jesus observed a lot just by looking at the people come in and give money.

It's significant that this story comes in Luke's Gospel immediately after Jesus' comment that the teachers of the law had been devouring widows' houses (Luke 20:47). People who considered themselves holy were swallowing up widows' resources! But in this situation, one very poor widow came to the temple and gave what she could.

Let's look at this story from a viewpoint other than the usual one—trying to get you to give more money. (But if you are led to do so, your church will accept it!) Jesus certainly never criticized the wealthy for their gifts. He didn't say that they ought to give more. In fact, in Mark's account of this event, he specifically states that the wealthy gave much (Mark 12:41). So Jesus was not condemning what the other people were doing; He was commending a woman whose sacrifice was great. This lesson, then, is not about stewardship, but about the motivation of the heart.

*Flash*Points

1. As Jesus looked at the people giving their money, what did He also look at (Mark 2:8)? Is this something Jesus always looked at?

2. As you read this chapter, consider this question: What are your honest thoughts as you give money to God?

Jesus Notices What We Call Little

What might we have noticed if we sat beside Jesus in the temple? First, we would have seen how Jesus noticed things we might call "little." Often the little things in life escape our notice. We are not conscious of them and their importance. Jesus looked at the widow's small gift and said it was the biggest gift of the day.

The woman gave only "two very small copper coins." They are called leptons, which means "thin ones." They were worth about half a penny, but it was all she had. We often do not take notice of the small things that people contribute because we don't realize that what seems small by human standards is often significant in God's eyes. Jesus commended this "small gift," because He knew exactly what it was worth.

Little things *do* make a difference. For instance, the quality of your family life will not be determined as much by the big decisions you make but by the everyday little decisions. How do you speak to your spouse and children? Do they hold a place of priority in the use of your time? Are you an encourager or a discourager? These things mount up and make a big, big difference.

One person who discovered that little things can make a difference was a test pilot out of Edwards Air Force Base. His plane flew by use of elaborate computer equipment, and one day when one of the relays went bad, he was afraid his plane might go down. He began a frantic search for something—anything—that could replace that relay. He found a paper clip, unbent it, and used it to connect the very sophisticated computer relays. That little paper clip, which was worth almost nothing in terms of money, was worth very much to that pilot that day. Little things do mean a lot.

*Flash*Points

1. What seemingly little things have meant a lot to you over the years?

2. What made those little things so meaningful?

3. What, in general, infuses small things with great meaning?

Jesus Blesses What We Call Little

Jesus often blesses those things we think are little. He can take a small gift and magnify it. He took this woman's small gift and used it to plant an idea in our minds about our own sacrifice. Even if you give something small to God, watch and see what dramatic things happen. Someone has calculated that if the widow's mite had been invested with even a modest return, at approximately four percent, today it would be worth $48 sextillion—that's 48 with twenty-one zeroes behind it! When I was a kid we would call that a "gazillion" dollars! It is impressive that the widow's mite would be worth that much if it had been invested, but what is the worth of her example? How can we calculate the character value of the number of people who have been inspired to greater generosity by the widow's mite, or calculate the worth of the lives that have been made better because of the generosity of Christians throughout the centuries? There is no question that on the spiritual level the widow's mite is worth more than can ever be calculated. God has taught us not to worry about what somebody else gives, or worry about the size of the gift—it is really the size of your heart that matters.

What do you have to give? Look at your life—money is actually minor. What do you have to offer the Lord and His kingdom? Your talent may seem like two small thin coins to you, but it may look like 48 sextillion dollars to God. But you must give it to Him before He can use it.

There once was a little girl who wanted to give something to missions. All she had was a penny, so she mailed that penny to a missionary in what was then Burma (now Myanmar). The missionary in Burma thought her gift was kind of cute, so he said, "I'll do something with it." He bought a tract with the penny and gave it to the chief of a tribe in Burma. The chief couldn't read, but was curious about what the tract said, so he walked over 250 miles to find somebody who could translate it. He believed what was in the tract and brought back the ideas to his tribe. They later invited missionaries to come to that village and teach them about Christ—all because a little girl gave just a penny. It didn't seem like a big gift at the time, but God turned it into something huge.

Another story involves a college in Georgia founded by a woman who wanted to make sure that a higher education was available to anyone who needed or wanted it. She often talked to people about underwriting some of the college's programs. She visited a very wealthy man who was in a bad mood that day. He didn't have much use for a new college, so he reached into his pocket and gave her a few cents. She said, "Thank you very much," and left. With his tiny gift, the woman bought seed. The students raised produce from that seed, sold it, and made more money. So she went back and told the gentleman, "I want you to see what we did with your investment." When he saw what they had done, he was ashamed of his small gift and eventually became one of the best supporters of that college. It's amazing what God can do with a small gift.

*Flash*Points

1. Has God taken something small in your life and by multiplying it over time made it into something more valuable?

2. How would the story about the little girl's gift of a penny have turned out differently if the missionary had had a cynical heart?

3. How would the story of the woman who opened the college have been different if she had scoffed at the wealthy man's offering?

We might ask the questions, "Should this widow have given away her last cent? If this was really all that she had, did God really expect her to give it away?" What God expects from us and what He accepts can be illustrated with this story.

Stu Weber said that one of his sons felt that he was the low man on the totem pole in the family. Everyone else in the family had something about them that was significant, but this boy felt that he was insignificant. Because this son liked the outdoors, Stu decided to give him a pocket knife. It was one of those knives that can do just about anything. All of a sudden this boy became quite a man of interest in the family. His self esteem was raised. On Stu Weber's birthday, he opened a present from this son and discovered that he had given back the very pocket knife that had brought him so much joy. Did Stu want to accept that gift? No, but he did, because he knew what it meant to his son to give back to his father what was most precious to him. If you are a parent, you probably don't need the gifts your children give you. You've got enough money to buy them yourself, but you accept them because of your children's desire to give, and you are grateful for their generosity and thoughtfulness.

My father told me about a time he visited missionaries in Africa. After he preached, the villagers gave him a gift for his services—a live duck. Now, that gave him pause. What would he do with a live duck? How would he get it home? But above all, he thought about how this gift was a significant sacrifice for these people. They didn't have much. So he leaned over to the missionary and said, "I can't accept this gift." The missionary said, "You must accept this gift. You have no right to deny them the privilege of giving." So my father did accept it and thanked the villagers for it. (In case you're wondering what happened to the duck, he gave it to the missionary.) But that missionary was right. These people gave out of their love and loyalty to Christ. Recognizing that, my father accepted their gift.

And God accepts our gifts. What is it that God really wants? Does God want our money? Of course, the church must operate on money. Mission work cannot be done without money. But most of all God wants us. Our money means a lot to us because we work hard for it and depend on it for so much. If we give God our money, we probably will not deny Him anything else. That's why our attitude toward wealth is an indicator of our commitment level. But what Jesus really wants is us—100 percent of us.

Have you ever noticed that God seems to enjoy people who are somewhat reckless in their love and in their faith? On one occasion, a woman broke an alabaster jar of expensive perfume and anointed Jesus' feet with the fragrant oil. The disciples commented that they could have fed the poor if they had sold the perfume. But Jesus said not to take away what she had done, that she would be an example for years to come (Matthew 26:6-13). That kind of abandonment in giving is precious. It is something Jesus delighted in seeing. Jesus didn't refuse to accept her extravagant gift.

The best gift to give somebody is a gift they want. We accept gifts even if they're not what we want, but the best gift is the one a person wants. Admittedly, we men are not always good at figuring out what women want. One time I thought I really had a gift figured out. My wife's aching feet had been bothering her for several months, so for Christmas I got her a very romantic gift—a footbath. You fill it with water and it heats the water and vibrates to massage the feet. I thought, *All right! I have gotten the gift of a lifetime for my wife!* She used it only once. Nevertheless, she thanked me for it and said, "You listened to me and heard my needs." Even though the gift itself was a disappointment, she appreciated the thought behind it.

*Flash*Points

1. Behind the gifts of the widow, Stu Weber's son, and the villagers in Africa was an enormous desire to give. What prompts such a desire?

2. Do you think this statement is accurate: "If we give God our money, we probably will not deny God anything else"? Why or why not?

3. The author's wife valued his gift because it meant he was listening to her. What does that have to do with the value of the gift?

Jesus Redefines What We Call Little

Others may have thought the widow's gift was little, but Jesus saw it as great because it came from an open heart. It was a big gift because she was willing to sacrifice self. It was an enormous gift because she gave out of her poverty.

A widow's life in the first century was very difficult. There were no government welfare programs or benevolence agencies. Many widows had to eke out a living. This woman evidently did that, but she still desired to give. How tough must it have been for the Father to accept that gift, but He did.

Jesus seemed to feel a kinship with this woman, perhaps because she mirrored the kind of love Jesus has for us. She, like Jesus, gave herself unreservedly and completely. Jesus went all the way to the cross for us. He was willing to sacrifice His life for us. Jesus saw in this woman the same kind of love. This widow's gift is often called the "widow's mite," but it's just as much a story of a "widow's might" because of the thought and heart behind it.

When King David was commanded by God to build an altar on the threshing floor of Araunah the Jebusite, David approached Araunah to buy the threshing floor. Araunah replied that he would simply give David whatever he required, including the oxen for the burnt offering and the threshing sledges and ox yokes for wood. David insisted on paying Araunah for everything, saying, "I will not sacrifice to the Lord my God burnt offerings that cost me nothing" (2 Samuel 24:24). It is true that this widow's gift cost her a lot. When you give your life to Christ, it will cost you a lot as well. It will cost you everything. When you come to Christ, you don't just give part of yourself to Him. You give all of yourself to Him.

Archibald Hart tells a wonderful story in *Habits of the Mind,* a story he heard from Og Mandino. The Durer brothers, Albrecht and Albert, worked for their father, who was a goldsmith. The father noticed that they had great artistic talent and he wanted them to develop their skill and become artists. But he could not afford to send them both to school. The two brothers discussed what they might do. They finally decided that one of them would work in the mines to help pay the way for the other to go to school and develop his artistic skill. Then that brother would return the favor. But which brother would go to school first? They flipped a coin. Albrecht won the coin toss. So he went off to school to study art, painting and sculpture.

After four years, Albrecht came home. As they sat together at dinner, Albrecht said to his brother Albert, "Now it's your turn. We can support you." But Albert looked up mournfully and held up his hands. Every one of his fingers had been broken at least once working in the mine. They were gnarled and stiff and useless for the fine work necessary from an artist. Albert said, "It's too late for me." But he told his brother, "You go, and you do it for both of us."

Albrecht appreciated Albert's sacrifice so much that he devised a tribute to his brother. You probably have seen Albrecht Durer's sculpture, "The Praying Hands." The hands in that sculpture are the gnarled hands of his brother, Albert. That's what it takes—sacrificing what is precious to us. Maybe we would have never known the genius of Albrecht Durer if it hadn't been for the sacrifice of his brother, Albert.

*Flash*Points

1. What important items might the widow have purchased instead of giving the money to God?

2. Can you think of a time when you, like the widow, have given yourself "unreservedly and completely"?

3. How would you describe the "might" of the widow?

4. David's words, "I will not sacrifice to the Lord my God burnt offerings that cost me nothing" indicate not only an enormous heart, but a clean heart. Why is integrity important in giving to God?

5. How is your appreciation of the sculpture, "The Praying Hands," enhanced by knowing the story behind it?

At this point, somebody might be thinking, *But I am a little person. What do I have to offer God? Why does God want me?* Maybe you think the gift of yourself is insignificant. I've talked to a lot of people who believe that. They ask, "How can God accept me with all the sins I've committed?" Or, "How can God use me? I have so few talents." Or, "How can I make a difference? I don't have a lot of power or authority." Many people in this world think they don't matter. They don't think God wants them or can use them, but surely this widow's gift shows us that God accepts our lives as they are and uses us for His purpose.

Remember: God delights in accepting what we consider a small gift and magnifying it! Who knows what God can do with you, with your gift, with your talent, with your time—if you just let Him. Go ahead and give God that small gift. You may find it turns out to be a much greater gift than you think.

The fact is, God wants you. Reinhold Niebuhr, the theologian, wrote a prayer that illustrates this great thought.

> Oh Lord, who has taught us that to gain the whole world and to lose our souls is great folly, grant us the grace so to lose ourselves that we may truly find ourselves anew in the life of grace, and so to forget ourselves that we may be remembered in your kingdom.

What do you have to give? You may think it's small, but in God's eyes there is no such thing as a small gift. For with

God's divine mathematics, He can transform any gift far beyond our ability to imagine. God notices little things. God commends little things. God magnifies little things. God redefines what it means to be little because "little" in the world's eyes is often great in God's eyes. Perhaps when you were little, you sang the song, "This Little Light of Mine." Maybe your light is little and it's all you have to offer. But use that light and . . . let it shine, let it shine, let it shine!

Warmed by the Light

Eight

Nicknames are funny things. Sometimes we name people exactly the opposite of what seems appropriate. For example, we may call a big man "Tiny." I've met some people with peculiar nicknames. In a community where I once served, there was a man whose first name was, "Pig." At least that's what I thought his first name was. Everybody always called him "Pig." "Hello, Pig," they would say.

One day I got the courage to ask, "Why does everyone call him 'Pig'?"

And people said, "When he was a young man in school, he had a pet pig. One day that pig followed him to school, so everybody started calling him 'Pig' and he's been called that ever since."

Isn't that a terrible twist of fate? One day a pig follows you to school and you're called "Pig" the rest of your life.

At a different church I served, there was a man we all knew as "Squire." He had earned this nickname by his dignified behavior. He was a leader in the church. He had a noble bearing. "Squire" fit him well.

A lot of people are known best by their nicknames. For instance, one of the church fathers is known as "Chrysostom." His real name was John, but in historical literature, he's called "Chrysostom," which means "golden mouth." It was a tribute to his abilities as a preacher. The first Prime Minister of Israel was known as "Ben-Gurion," but his real name was David Green. He was called "Ben-Gurion," which means "son of the lion." Even Buddha was not known by his real name. Buddha means "enlightened one," but the man's real name was Siddhartha.

In Scripture, we find a man best-known by his nickname. His real name was Joseph. Now, there are many famous Josephs in the Bible—the favored son of Jacob sold as a slave into Egypt, the earthly father of our Lord Jesus, and the Jewish council leader, who gave his tomb for the burial of Jesus, to name a few. The Joseph we want to study today was a Levite from Cypress, who is known in history by his nickname, Barnabas.

What does "Barnabas" mean? It can mean several things such as "son of prophecy" or "son of exhortation" or "con-solation." It was interpreted by Luke and the others who knew Barnabas to mean "son of encouragement." What a great nickname to have!

What would be your nickname if people decided to name you by the dominant characteristic of your life? Would some of us be known as "Mr. Angry" or "Ms. Depressed" or "Mr. Stingy" or "Ms. Dishonest"? Wouldn't it be wonderful if people found something really nice about us and that became our nickname?

When farm animals need to be kept warm, lights in the stalls are turned on to produce warmth. When we are in the cold, dark grip of discouragement and despair, sincere words of encouragement can bring light to our path and restore warmth to our hearts. Let's take a look at how Barnabas shared his warming light of encouragement with others.

*Flash*Points

1. What is the most unusual nickname you can recall?

2. What is the most fitting nickname you can recall?

3. What nickname would you most like to have that reflects a godly character?

Caring for the Needy

One of the ways Barnabas was an encourager was by giving away his goods.

All the believers were one in heart and mind. No one claimed that any of his possessions was his own, but they shared everything they had. With great power the apostles continued to testify to the resurrection of the Lord Jesus, and much grace was upon them all. There were no needy persons among them. For from time to time those who owned lands or houses sold them, brought the money from the sales and put it at the apostles' feet, and it was distributed to anyone as he had need.

Joseph, a Levite from Cyprus, whom the apostles called Barnabas (which means Son of Encouragement), sold a field he owned and brought the money and put it at the apostles' feet. Acts 4:32-37

You may wonder how Barnabas could give this extraordinary gift of land since Levites weren't supposed to own property. Once the Levites went out into the Hellenistic world, some of the restrictions that were upon the Levites who lived in Jerusalem seem to have been relaxed. Also a Levite could own land for the purposes of burial, so maybe this was a burial plot. Barnabas's gift inspired others in the early church to give so that "there were no needy persons among them."

Fred Craddock says there are only two ways to have a congregation like that. One is to keep your membership requirements so strict that needy people are kept out of the church. The other is to take care of those needs.

Some denominations that no longer believe in evangelism often specialize in benevolence. This happens because once you no longer believe in a need for personal salvation, all that is left for the church to do is good, practical deeds. On the other hand, it is equally as wrong for evangelistic churches to forget benevolence. Evangelism and benevolence go hand in hand. Souls live in bodies and often the body must be ministered to first. How can you save a soul if the body it dwells in dies of starvation? Jesus, who told us to go into the world and preach the gospel, also told us to give a cup of cold water, to clothe those who are naked, and to visit those who are in prison (Matthew 10:42; 25:31-46). If you take the first commandment seriously, you ought to take the second just as seriously. It's important to continue the ministry of benevolence by blessing people who have physical needs.

*Flash*Points

1. How easy do you find it to be an encourager by giving gifts, maybe even small gifts?
   __ easy
   __ somewhat easy
   __ somewhat difficult
   __ difficult

2. Which do you tend to rate more highly: offering words of encouragement or giving gifts of encouragement? Why?

3. How do you go about helping someone who is needy and doing it as an encourager, not as an awkward do-gooder?

Mentoring New Believers

When Saul, a devoted enemy of the cause of Christ, turned around and became a Christian, people were suspicious of him. Maybe they assumed he was spying on them. At first no one wanted to have much to do with him, but take a look at what Barnabas did.

> But Barnabas took him and brought him to the apostles. He told them how Saul on his journey had seen the Lord and that the Lord had spoken to him, and how in Damascus he had preached fearlessly in the name of Jesus. So Saul stayed with them and moved about freely in Jerusalem, speaking boldly in the name of the Lord.   Acts 9:27, 28

Barnabas was willing to vouch for Saul's transformed character. Have you ever been asked to be put on a job seeker's reference list? Have you ever been asked to vouch for someone's character? That's risky business. It was no small thing for Barnabas to take Saul to meet the apostles. Seven years later, Barnabas brought Paul to Antioch and even put him on his staff as his associate minister. Barnabas was a man who was willing to mentor others.

In the book, *The Other Twelve,* Leslie Flynn compares Charles Colson to Saul. When Colson became a believer, many people thought, *Right! He found the Lord in prison. Everybody finds the Lord in prison.* People didn't want much to do with Colson because he was known as Nixon's hatchet man. He was a tough man and was often involved in dirty tricks. Then Harold Hughes invited Colson to his Bible study and prayer group. While there, Colson saw a man he had once played a dirty trick on. During the meeting, Harold Hughes got up and gave a testimony about giving up hatreds. He said, "One man I used to hate was Charles Colson, but I have brought him to you today as a Christian brother and I want you to welcome him." At the end of the Bible study, the man Colson had played the dirty trick on was asked to pray. He came over and grasped Colson's hand as they formed a prayer circle. Colson recalls what an extraordinary experience it was to be accepted into that circle. But it never would have happened if Harold Hughes had not had the courage to be a Barnabas and bring him in.

*Flash*Points

1. If someone comes alongside a former enemy in a gesture of encouragement and acceptance, what often happens in the heart of the enemy?

2. What character qualities are required to sincerely encourage someone who has wronged you?

3. How does this sort of behavior imitate Christ?

Encouraging the Outcasts

We also see Barnabas as an encourager. When the leaders of the Jerusalem church learned about the things happening in the church of Antioch, they were worried. The Antioch church was growing, but they were bringing in all these Greek Gentiles who didn't know what to bring to a church supper! The Greeks didn't know how to say prayer right and didn't know the songs. To the church in Jerusalem, it was a terrible, worrisome thing. And so they decided to send an emissary. They wanted someone to assess the situation, teach the new Christians, and bless the church. They chose Barnabas to do it.

> When he arrived and saw the evidence of the grace of God, he was glad and encouraged them all to remain true to the Lord with all their hearts. He was a good man, full of the Holy Spirit and faith, and a great number of people were brought to the Lord.

Then Barnabas went to Tarsus to look for Saul, and when he found him, he brought him to Antioch. So for a whole year Barnabas and Saul met with the church and taught great numbers of people. The disciples were called Christians first at Antioch.   Acts 11:23-26

The church in Antioch invited Barnabas, who had urged them to remain true to the Lord with all their hearts, to preach there. He agreed to come, but first went to Tarsus to get Paul and brought him back as an associate. The two of them developed the first ministry to the Gentile world. Barnabas was what we might call a liaison. He had a vision to win the Gentiles and was willing to break down some of the barriers that previously he had accepted.

Perhaps you've heard this story about the early days of the Billy Graham crusades. Sometimes the crusade would go into a city where segregation was the law. Blacks and whites could not sit together. Rather than challenge segregation or not go at all, Billy Graham would schedule the crusade but right before the meeting began, he would personally walk through the crowd and remove the barriers. Who was going to tell him he couldn't? In that way, he was telling people who had been shut out and treated as outcasts that they were accepted by God.

We may take inclusion for granted now, but it was a major concern to the early church. So much so that they had to have a conference to decide how to deal with all these people from different backgrounds who were joining the church. Barnabas was one of the first to accept them and to bless them, and that was an encouragement.

*Flash*Points

1. How did Barnabas go out of his way to help Saul?

2. The early church experienced cultural differences in the worship styles of the Jewish and Gentile believers. What message does this have for us?

3. What sorts of people are excluded—the needy, the elderly, the handicapped—whom you particularly enjoy encouraging?

4. How did Jesus encourage the excluded?

Encouraging the Failures

When Barnabas and Paul went on their first missionary journey, they took a young man with them by the name of John Mark. John Mark was evidently a relative of Barnabas. He was a promising young believer, but for reasons we don't know, John Mark went home about halfway through the journey. Many have speculated that John Mark abandoned the mission because he lacked courage, but there are a hundred reasons why he might have left. Maybe he got homesick. Maybe he didn't like the rigors of the itinerant life—ministering from place to place. Maybe he just missed his family and friends. Maybe he didn't like watching all "those Gentiles" come into the church. Some have even suggested that he didn't like what was happening in relation to Barnabas and Paul. When the missionary journey started, the two were referred to as "Barnabas and Saul" (Acts 11:26, 30; 12:25; 13:2, 7), but Luke later changed the order to "Paul and Barnabas" (Acts 13:42, 43, 46, 50; 14:1, 3, 23; 15:2, 22, 35). That change in name order may indicate a change in who was perceived as the leader. Paul began to be recognized as more important than Barnabas. Possibly that bothered John Mark.

Barnabas was evidently physically taller than Paul. We don't know if that means he was a big man or just big in comparison to Paul. On one occasion, when they came into a village and did miracles, the villagers called them Zeus and Hermes (Acts 14:12). In Greek mythology, Zeus was the father of all the gods. They pointed to Barnabas and said he was Zeus. They thought Paul was Hermes. Hermes was the messenger of the gods—the one pictured with the wings on his feet that we see in the F.T.D. florist ads. Paul was the talker, so they figured he must be the messenger. At the beginning of their trip, Barnabas was the senior minister and Paul was the associate, but it seems that later, Paul became the senior minister.

One of the joys and privileges of working at a church

with a multiple staff is working with talented people. But I wonder what I would do if my church asked me to relinquish preaching responsibilities to one of my associate ministers? Could I say, "All right, you will now be the senior minister and I will be your associate?" I have to be honest and tell you I don't think I could do that. I'm not like Barnabas. I couldn't do that, but Barnabas could. There's no indication he ever resented Paul, but perhaps John Mark did.

When it came time to travel again, Barnabas wanted to give John Mark a second chance, but Paul said no because John Mark had deserted them before. It's interesting that Paul wouldn't give John Mark a second chance after he himself had been given one. A great disagreement developed.

> Barnabas wanted to take John, also called Mark, with them, but Paul did not think it wise to take him, because he had deserted them in Pamphylia and had not continued with them in the work. They had such a sharp disagreement that they parted company. Barnabas took Mark and sailed for Cyprus, but Paul chose Silas and left, commended by the brothers to the grace of the Lord.   Acts 15:37-40

Notice it was a "sharp disagreement." This was no small argument. As a result, they went their separate ways. The Lord used this division, however, because then there were two teams to win others to the Lord.

But Barnabas was right about John Mark, and later Paul described John Mark as someone who was very useful to him (2 Timothy 4:11). John Mark was one of the people who encouraged Paul when he was in prison in Rome. There are many times when we are in a position to help give someone a second chance.

In one of my early ministries, I felt people weren't responding well. I got a lot of criticism, and it was a tough time. I decided to leave the ministry. I wrote my resignation letter and brought it to the chairman of the elders. He very quietly read my letter all the way through and then, without saying a word, he folded it, tore it up and threw it in the trash can. He said, "I refuse to accept this letter. If we're not responding to the preaching of the Word, it's our fault, not yours. If you want to find another church, find another church. If you want to stay with us, stay with us. But don't leave the ministry." The elder continued, "Don't leave a mark like that on the record of this church. We don't want to drive a good man out of the ministry." People like him were in my life whenever I needed that kind of encouragement— the kind that Barnabas offered.

*Flash*Points

1. When have you been grateful for a second chance?

2. In what concrete ways can we encourage those who need second chances?

3. What sort of inner character would a person need to let a colleague, once subordinate, now move ahead?

All of us need someone like Barnabas, who was a mentor to many. We need someone who is willing to believe in us. I experienced that in high school when I was very insecure. I tried sports. I wasn't very good at sports and failed at that. I tried to get elected to office in the student government. I lost the election. I was really floundering. What was I going to do? Then a drama teacher saw potential in me and cast me for a major role in the first play I ever auditioned for. That flabbergasted me, but I gave it my best. I ended up being in drama for the rest of my high school and college years. That teacher helped me acquire the confidence that otherwise I would not have had.

A lot of what's happening in men's ministry right now centers around mentoring. But in some communities, there are groups that are attended mostly by younger men and other groups attended mostly by more senior men. The younger men don't know why the senior men don't want to spend time with them, and the senior men wonder why the young guys don't want to spend time with them. The fact is that the senior men have advice and counsel and support to offer the younger men. If those two groups got together, they would both have to bend a little bit, but it would be worth it. We need each other.

Let me tell you about a young man who grew up in Hazard County, Kentucky. A fellow who was a part-time minister and a part-time salve salesman began encouraging this young man to go into the ministry. You probably have never heard of the part-time salve salesman, but the young man he encouraged to go into the ministry was E. Ray (Cotton) Jones. Cotton has had several successful ministries, and you many have read articles written by him. Cotton went into the ministry because a mature man of God encouraged him.

I think of another man. The woman he would marry was invited to church by her schoolteacher. There she was led to the Lord. She, in turn, led him to the Lord and they were married. One day the preacher in that church asked him to fill in on a Sunday night. He did that. A local church who couldn't find a preacher asked him to fill in for them, so he did. He decided that maybe he should get an education, so while he was preaching he went to college. He finished his education and he is now preaching at the Valley View Christian Church in Dallas, Texas. This large church gives a half a million dollars every year to missions. His name is Dennis Slaughter and he was the 1998 President of the North American Christian Convention. His ministry began with that teacher who had that first opportunity to be an encourager, and the minister who first asked him to preach.

When my wife and I were on vacation, we visited Plains, Georgia, to see the Jimmy Carter Museum. It's housed in a school building. As soon as you walk into the building, you see the former principal's office. On the walls are tributes to her from all her students, including ones from Jimmy and Rosalynn Carter. Jimmy Carter wrote that the principal was the one who gave him the courage to think that a boy from Plains, Georgia, could become President of the United States.

*Flash*Points

1. Who has been a mentor to you—perhaps informally, but nevertheless a mentor?

2. Mentoring often occurs between people in similar settings of some kind—colleagues at work, neighbors, coworkers on a church committee. In what settings might God call you to mentor someone?

3. If you mentored someone, how would you pray for him or her?

You never know what your encouraging word might do for someone because it often bears fruit long after the seed was planted. When Barnabas first began to be an encourager,

I'm sure he didn't know what would be the outcome of his work. I want to encourage you to be like Barnabas. Be a good person, filled with the Holy Spirit and with faith. We can all become sons and daughters of encouragement.

Nine
Emergency Light

One of my favorite musicals is *Camelot*, which is based on the book, *The Once and Future King*. I can't watch the closing scene without being moved. As King Arthur sees his utopian Camelot coming to an end, he finds a young page and tells him of all the great dreams he had, and the wonderful moments Camelot enjoyed. Arthur tells the page to go back to England and tell the story. "Ask every person if they've heard the story. And tell it strong and clear if they have not." He wants the page to explain that for one brief, shining moment there was a place known as Camelot, a place of perfect peace and harmony.

Some mistakenly think that the early church had a Camelot experience, that for one brief, shining moment in history, everything was perfect and everyone got along. But that is simply not true. From its inception, the church experienced persecution and death. At the beginning of today's lesson text, the apostle James was martyred and at the end of it, prison guards were executed (Acts 12:2, 19). In between, Peter was miraculously delivered from jail.

The church has suffered throughout the centuries, but we know now that persecution only makes faith grow. The true test of our faith is not how we respond when times are easy, but how we respond when times are tough. How do we keep shining God's light in the midst of chaos?

*Flash*Points

1. Why do you think people often have a romanticized view of the early church?

2. Based on what you've read above, what four words would you use to more accurately describe life in the early church?

3. How does this view help us understand Scripture more accurately?

Rhoda was a servant girl in the household of John Mark's family. Her life in that household must have been interesting, for some Bible scholars suggest that this was the house in which the disciples gathered for the upper room experience. It may also have been the house in which the Holy Spirit came upon the apostles in a miraculous way at Pentecost (Acts 2), although some scholars believe this event may have occurred in an area of the temple. In Acts 12, we see that the church met there to pray for Peter. When their prayers were miraculously answered and Peter was released from prison, he made his way back to the church, gathered in John Mark's house. Then a rather humorous event occurred.

> When this had dawned on him, he went to the house of Mary the mother of John, also called Mark, where many people had gathered and were praying. Peter knocked at the outer entrance, and a servant girl named Rhoda came to answer the door. When she recognized Peter's voice, she was so overjoyed she ran back without opening it and exclaimed, "Peter is at the door!"
>
> "You're out of your mind," they told her. When she kept insisting that it was so, they said, "It must be his angel."
>
> But Peter kept on knocking, and when they opened the door and saw him, they were astonished. Peter motioned with his hand for them to be quiet and described how the Lord had brought him out of prison. "Tell James and the brothers about this," he said, and then he left for another place.
>
> In the morning, there was no small commotion among the soldiers as to what had become of Peter. After Herod had a thorough search made for him and did not find him, he cross-examined the guards and ordered that they be executed.
>
> Acts 12:12-19

Rhoda must have seen experienced a lot in that household. We don't know whether she was a believer or not, but we do know that she was excited when Peter was released. No doubt she had some strong feelings about those church people. We don't even know whether she was one of them, and yet she shows us an example of a simple acceptance of answered prayer that even the Christians in the household didn't have.

Let's look at this incident through Rhoda's eyes to see how we can develop the kind of trust she had.

She Saw the Church in Community

First, she saw the church gathered at that house to worship. She saw their habits, their attitudes, their actions, and the quality of their worship service. She saw how they treated each other. She saw how they treated outsiders. She saw the dynamic fellowship and benevolence of that early church. She saw the power of the Holy Spirit working mightily in them when they were in crisis. And she saw how they treated her—a servant—personally. Did Rhoda formulate opinions of Christians—and of Christ—based on what she saw? Sometimes we don't realize how much people judge Christ on the basis of what they see when they come to church. There is so much we can do for the cause of Christ if we live as we ought to live. No matter what else we may think of a church, we are generally going to judge it by how its members treat us personally. Someone once said that there would be more Christians if the church acted more like Christ.

We may assume that Rhoda had a favorable impression of the church, but she saw more than just the good stuff.

She Saw the Church in Crisis

As the maidservant in John Mark's household, Rhoda may have met Jesus. If she did, she no doubt felt attracted to Him. Jesus' arrest and death on the cross—whether she witnessed it or not and whether or not she understood its significance—was probably a big disappointment for her. As one who listened to the concerns of the church, she undoubtedly knew of the death of Stephen, the death of James, and the imprisonment of Peter.

She Saw the Church in Prayer

On this day, Rhoda was able to see an answer to the prayers of the church. She witnessed not just a church in community and in crisis, but also a church in prayer. And then she saw the church in triumph. However, this servant girl was more willing to quickly accept Peter's release than the leaders were. She received the answer to their prayers with great joy.

*Flash*Points

1. Do you agree or disagree that non-Christians form opinions of the church (and ultimately of Christ) based on how Christians treat one another, and how they treat people in service positions (waiters and hotel staff)?

2. If non-Christians are to visit a church service and recognize the presence of God, what kinds of things must the people in the pews be doing in regard to worship of God? In regard to how they treat visitors?

Earlier, Herod had put James in jail and then put him to death. Herod saw that James's death pleased the Jewish leaders and so he concluded that they would love it if he did the same to Peter. Herod arrested Peter and probably planned to kill him once the holidays were over. Peter was in prison, but God's people were earnestly praying for him.

> The night before Herod was to bring him to trial, Peter was sleeping between two soldiers, bound with two chains, and sentries stood guard at the entrance.
>
> Acts 12:6

She Saw the Church in Triumph

It took great faith for Peter not to worry all night. Even though the next day could bring his death sentence, he wasn't fretting—he was sleeping. Don't we wish we could have that kind of peace? We may also wonder how he could have slept in that uncomfortable circumstance, chained to soldiers in a prison cell. It seems that Peter was ready for whatever happened. Regardless of how it turned out, Peter had peace about his situation.

That night, God intervened.

> Suddenly an angel of the Lord appeared and a light shone in the cell. He struck Peter on the side and woke him up. "Quick, get up!" he said, and the chains fell off Peter's wrists.
>
> Then the angel said to him, "Put on your clothes and sandals." And Peter did so. "Wrap your cloak around you and follow me," the angel told him. Peter followed him out of the prison, but he had no idea that what the angel was doing was really happening; he thought he was seeing a vision.
>
> Acts 12:7-9

Did you notice that Peter was sleeping so soundly that the angel had to hit him to wake him up? Then the angel had to tell Peter to get dressed, apparently because he had been sleeping so soundly that he was groggy. Finally, when Peter reached the gate leading into the city and the gate opened by itself, he realized that his release was real. He went to the house of John Mark's mother and knocked on the door, and Rhoda was so happy to see him that she forgot to let him in! Peter had just escaped from prison and so he was in danger by being outside. Can you imagine how he felt? "Come on folks, let me in!" But they doubted it was he. Eventually Peter came in and met with the whole group.

*Flash*Points

1. What details of this miraculous event are most interesting to you?

2. During stressful times, what do you do at night to find enough peace with God so you can sleep?

Let's try to understand why these early Christians responded as they did. Why were they more ready to believe that Rhoda was crazy than that Peter had been released? In fact, they said to her, "You're out of your mind" (Acts

12:15). The Greek text uses only one word for this phrase. This one word might be translated as, "you crazy." They just looked at her and said, "You're crazy!"

Then this group of Christians conceded that perhaps Rhoda had seen Peter's angel—but still not Peter himself. What does that mean? Evidently some people believed that a person's guardian angel resembled that person. They were more ready to believe that an angel stood at the door than that Peter had been released. How often are you surprised when your prayers are answered?

The shock and disbelief at Peter's appearance has led some Bible students to think that the church wasn't even praying for Peter's release, but for his comfort in prison. That could be true. We don't know what they were praying for, but I hope that if I am ever arrested for my faith and put in jail, the church will not pray just for my comfort. Pray for me to get out of there!

My belief is that they were praying for Peter to get out of prison. What a blow the imprisonment of Peter must have been to the church! After all, they had just faced the severe loss of James, the apostle. To see another one of that inner circle of Jesus, the one who was "chairman of the executive committee" so to speak, in jail—most likely facing death—must have been frightening. Jesus had been executed. James had been executed. They had every reason to believe death would come to Peter, too. And so they prayed.

*Flash*Points

1. How does fear often affect our prayer?

2. How might Herod's authority to execute James have intimidated these Christians?

3. What causes you to be filled with doubt and fear in your prayer?
   ___ the death or severe punishment of someone
   ___ intimidating, powerful people
   ___ coming against a monolithic structure, such as a government
   ___ tiresomeness of long waiting
   ___ other:

You have to wonder how the church would have responded if Peter had faced the same fate as James. Would that have meant that God was not faithful to the prayers of the church? Many have wondered this in the past, but the topic is as fresh as this morning's newspaper.

As I am writing this, the news reports tell of an eleven-year-old boy and a fourteen-year-old boy in Jonesboro, Arkansas, who have shot and killed classmates out of anger. I'm sure that the parents of the children who survived were relieved to see their children alive and praised the Lord, but that does not mean that God was angry with the children who didn't survive or with their parents. God doesn't have to bring heartache into this world—it's here. People do terrible things out of their own free will. We can ask God, "Why didn't you stop it?" but God doesn't forcefully control His children. He didn't make this event happen, nor did He stop it. If we are going to question how evil can get into the heart of a couple of children who kill, we've also got to question how such goodness can get into the heart of a teacher that she would sacrifice her own life by standing in the line of fire to save a student. Why is there evil? Why is there good? Both were experienced in Jonesboro, Arkansas, that day.

If you are going through great trials yourself, you may be asking, "Why did God allow me to go through this? Why didn't God prevent this or that from happening?" I don't know why, but I know the answer is far beyond the question, "Are you angry with me, Lord?" Evil has nothing to do with whom God likes and doesn't like.

When talk show host Larry King interviewed Billy Graham, Graham talked about a man who prayed to get a seat on a certain plane so he could get home to his family. But he couldn't get on the flight he wanted—which later crashed and killed all who were aboard. Larry King asked Billy Graham, "Does that mean God was mad at everybody else on the plane? Does that mean God didn't like those people?" Graham said "no" and was quiet for a moment. Then he said, "All I mean is that we don't always know what to pray for. We don't always know what is right for us."

That's true, but Larry King asked a good question that many ask. Many of us have prayed very hard and have seen our prayers come true in dramatic ways. We have prayed equally hard at other times when it seems like nothing happened.

Some commentary writers believe James was martyred because the church failed to pray for him, but Peter wasn't because they did pray for him. I reject that idea even though I've seen it mentioned several times. Why? Because my experience tells me that it's not always how hard I pray that makes a difference.

I don't believe things happened the way they did because God favored Peter and didn't favor James. It may be that God intervened in Peter's case because the church could not have handled another loss of leadership. According to tradition, Peter eventually did die a martyr's death, so he didn't escape it, he just postponed it. We don't know why God spared him, but we can praise God for sparing Peter and at the same time celebrate the martyrdom of James. The answers are beyond our ability to see and to understand.

We can see many examples of this. For instance, God did not bring the trouble that came into Job's life. Admittedly, God did not prevent it, but He did not bring it into Job's life. God did not put into the mind of Judas to do the terrible thing he did to Jesus, but neither did God stop it. God did not place into the heart of Herod the murderous thoughts to kill the apostles. God prevented the murder of one apostle, but not the other.

Consider the predicament of Jesus in Gethsemane. His prayer was, "My Father, if it is possible, may this cup be taken from me. Yet not as I will, but as you will" (Matthew 26:39). Notice how Jesus phrased His request, "if it is possible." Jesus asked that He not have to endure the cross, but God, with His infinite wisdom, knew that the request could not be granted. We have to accept the fact that some of our prayers are simply not going to be answered in the way that we hope. Job never did get his answer as to why all those catastrophes happened to him. His basic answer from God was something like this, "I can't explain it to you because you couldn't understand it."

In my own life, my wife and I have dealt with the pain of infertility. We prayed a lot to conceive children but it has never happened. Yet, I have prayed for several others in the same situation and those couples have since had children. I have said, "Lord, I don't understand why You've granted my prayers for children for others, but You haven't granted them for me." That is a difficult question. At the same time, God has been kind to me in other ways. My wife and I have been blessed with the special joys of adoption. I might just as well ask, "God, why have you blessed us so much with this wonderful daughter?" There are times in our lives when we need to say, "OK, God, I can't understand your will, I don't

always agree with your answers, but I know you love me."
We may never understand "why," but we must always keep
praying. I do know from experience that great things happen
when people pray, even if the answers aren't exactly what
we prayed for.

*Flash*Points

1. If God is not responsible for the evil in this world, who
   is? (See 2 Thessalonians 2:1-10; James 1:13-15)

2. Why do we so quickly suppose that God is angry with us
   when things go wrong?

3. Why can it be helpful to say to God, "Lord, I don't
   understand why you've granted my prayers for other
   people but you haven't granted them for me"?

4. When is it not helpful to ask that question?

We Don't Have to Know All the Answers

A lot of us, I suppose, share the faith of a little child who was staying with her grandfather. He was happy to see her praying at night, kneeling by her bed. But the words coming out of her mouth were unusual. She was saying, A, B, C, D, E, F, G, H, I, J. When she finished praying, her grandfather said, "Honey I was glad to see you praying, but why were you reciting the alphabet?" She said, "I don't really know what to say, so I just say the letters and I let God put the words together." Sometimes that is exactly what we have to do. And we have to accept the fact that sometimes God says no.

Claudia Minden Welsz wrote these words:

> I asked God to take away my pride, and God said no.
> He said it was not for Him to take away, but for me to give it up.
> I asked God to make my handicapped child whole, and God said no.
> He said the child's spirit is whole; the body is only temporary.
> I asked God to grant me patience, and God said no.
> He said that patience is a byproduct of tribulation. It isn't granted, it is earned.
> I asked God to give happiness, and God said no.
> He said He gives me blessings; happiness is up to me.
> I asked God to spare me pain, and God said no.

He said, "Suffering draws you apart from worldly cares and brings you closer to me."

I asked God to make my spirit grow, and God said no.

He said I must grow my own, but He will prune me to make me fruitful.

I asked God if He loved me, and God said yes.

He gave me His only Son who died for me and I'll be in heaven some day because I believe.

I asked God to help me love others as much as He loves me, and God said, "Ah finally, finally you have the idea."

While I don't propose to give you all the answers here, I do want you to see that this seeming paradox in prayer has been experienced by a lot of people. A lot of the heroes of the Bible experienced it. Paul was able to heal others and yet after three occasions of deep prayer over his own thorn in the flesh, God said, "My grace is sufficient for you, for my power is made perfect in weakness" (2 Corinthians 12:9). We will all experience these things, but we know that in the end God will accomplish His will and make things turn out right.

Here is an example of how God makes things come out right when they seem unjust.

Then Herod went from Judea to Caesarea and stayed there a while. He had been quarreling with the people of Tyre and Sidon; they now joined together and sought an audience with him. Having secured the support of Blastus, a trusted personal servant of the king, they asked for peace, because they depended on the king's country for their food supply.

On the appointed day Herod, wearing his royal robes, sat on his throne and delivered a public address to the people. They shouted, "This is the voice of a god, not of a man." Immediately, because Herod did not give praise to God, an angel of the Lord struck him down, and he was eaten by worms and died.

But the word of God continued to increase and spread.

Acts 12:19-24

Eventually, Herod got what was coming to him. On this earth or in the next life, God balances the scales. When we see injustice, we may be tempted to say, "God cannot exist if there is injustice like this." Or we can say, "God must exist in order for us to handle injustice like this." It all depends on how we decide to look at it.

*Flash*Points

1. In what way does the child's response above ("I don't really know what to say, so I just say the letters and I let God put the words together") show trust?

2. When, if ever, have you felt the way this child did?

3. Circle the lines in the poem above that most closely resemble your experience with God.

4. How do you suppose the folks at John Mark's house responded to Herod's dramatic death?

I admire the way Rhoda simply accepted God's answer to prayer with great joy. That's a childlike quality, isn't it? Jesus said that if we want to be great in the kingdom, we have to be like a little child (Matthew 18:3, 4). We often see this unquestioning faith in children and in new believers. We can learn from their example. This is the kind of trust that can handle any emergency and any outcome. This trust can bless Peter and bless James and believe that God used both their lives and deaths for His glory.

This kind of faith was immortalized in the great hymn Martin Luther wrote,

> A mighty Fortress is our God, a Bulwark never failing.
> Our Helper He, amid the flood Of mortal ills prevailing:
> For still our ancient foe doth seek to work us woe;
> His craft and power are great, and, armed with cruel hate,
> On earth is not His equal.
> Did we in our own strength confide, our striving would be losing,
> Were not the right Man on our side, the Man of God's own choosing:
> Dost ask who that might be? Christ Jesus, it is He;
> Lord Sabaoth His name, from age to age the same,
> And He must win the battle.

And tho this world, with devils filled, should threaten to undo us;

We will not fear, for God hath willed His truth to triumph through us.

The Prince of Darkness grim, we tremble not for him;

His rage we can endure, for lo! his doom is sure,

One little word shall fell him.

The word, above all earthly powers, no thanks to them, abideth:

The spirit and the gifts are ours thro Him who with us sideth;

Let goods and kindred go, this mortal life also;

The body they may kill: God's truth abideth still;

His kingdom is forever.

Ten
Spotlight

Sudden realizations. They happen to all of us at one time or another. As students, we wrestle with a difficult math problem or a difficult scientific formula and suddenly the light bulb in the mind comes on. Not only do we see it, but we can't understand why we didn't see it earlier. A sudden realization. Or maybe you look in the mirror and realize, *My hair's gone gray!* Your spouse, of course, has been noticing it for quite a while, but it's a sudden realization to you.

Sudden realizations are part of the spiritual life as well. For some, sudden realizations lead to their conversion. For others, coming to Christ happens gradually because they've grown up in a Christian home. For all of us, deeper realizations of who Jesus is and what He wants of us occur throughout our life as we study the Word of God and continue to grow in knowledge of Him.

But do these realizations really happen that suddenly? The understanding of a math problem may seem to have occurred suddenly, but it required a great deal of patient teaching and explanation leading up to the realization. That hair was going gray all along, but you just didn't notice it.

*Flash*Points

1. What, if any, sudden realizations have you had recently —from your body, your memory, your friends? (For

example, you body may have nudged you to slow down.)

2. How did these nudges persuade you to change your behavior?

At first glance, the conversion of Saul seems to have occurred quite suddenly.

> Meanwhile, Saul was still breathing out murderous threats against the Lord's disciples. He went to the high priest and asked him for letters to the synagogues in Damascus, so that if he found any there who belonged to the Way, whether men or women, he might take them as prisoners to Jerusalem. As he neared Damascus on his journey, suddenly a light from heaven flashed around him. He fell to the ground and heard a voice say to him, "Saul, Saul, why do you persecute me?"
>
> "Who are you, Lord?" Saul asked.
>
> "I am Jesus, whom you are persecuting," he replied. "Now get up and go into the city, and you will be told what you must do."
>
> The men traveling with Saul stood there speechless; they heard the sound but did not see anyone. Saul got up from the ground, but when he opened his eyes he could see nothing. So they led him by the hand into Damascus. For three days he was blind, and did not eat or drink anything.   Acts 9:1-9

In the midst of his "murderous threats" against the church, Saul was struck blind. God's spotlight fell upon him. He fell to the ground and came face to face with the risen Lord. But when we take a closer look at what seems like a sudden conversion, we see that God had been setting the stage for some time.

When Saul told the story later, he recounted that one of the things Jesus said to him was, "It is hard for you to kick against the goads" (Acts 26:14). In other words, "I've been trying to prod you, or to use a goad to move you in the right direction, but you've been resisting." Later, Paul said that this event was not so much for his conversion as for his commission. (Acts 26:16). To be an apostle, you had to have witnessed the risen Lord. So that great light on the road to Damascus may have temporarily, physically blinded Saul, but it opened his heart and mind to things he had never seen before.

Besides the vision, which was of course a significant nudge, I wonder if the death of Stephen might have been a goad as well. Saul held the coats of the men who stoned Stephen to death (Acts 7:54—8:1). He didn't actually put his hand to kill Stephen, but he affirmed those who did. Perhaps as he watched, the attitude of Stephen—the brightness of his countenance, his courage, his peace—began to affect him.

There was also the influence of his mentor, Gamaliel. Saul had studied to be a rabbi under Gamaliel, the most famous teacher of his day. Gamaliel was a Pharisee, and a highly-respected teacher of the law. When Peter and the other apostles were on trial for preaching in the temple courts, Gamaliel warned the Sanhedrin to leave them alone. He said, "Men of Israel, consider carefully what you intend to do to these men. . . . For if their purpose or activity is of human origin, it will fail. But if it is from God, you will not be able to stop these men; you will only find yourselves fighting against God" (Acts 5:34-39). Whether or not Saul actually heard these words in person, we may safely assume that he discussed this new religion with his teacher and was fully aware of Gamaliel's warning. Don't you imagine that Gamaliel's warning shook the foundations of Saul's position against the church?

What about the example of all the people Saul had persecuted? Paul later affirmed that he had been responsible for the deaths of some Christians (Acts 26:9-11; 1 Timothy 1:13, 15, 16). Don't you imagine the commitment and courage of those he persecuted affected him? Maybe he began to think he wasn't their superior after all, but that they were his superiors. Perhaps he saw that he was not the man he wanted to be and that was a painful truth to discover.

*Flash*Points

1. Remembering that a "goad" is a nudge or prompting, why is it important to pay attention to the "goads" of God?

2. How can it be harmful to ignore these promptings?

3. What nudges has God been giving you lately, perhaps in the form of events in your life, someone's words, or the expression on someone's face?

Seeing Jesus Better

Anyone who has ever worn an eye patch will tell you how they quickly learned to depend on their other senses, and how the temporary blindness helped them think more deeply. We also marvel at how people who live with blindness develop keen memories, a superfine sense of touch, and use their sense of smell to identify substances. Perhaps during Saul's period of blindness, he thought more deeply. One thing he certainly saw clearly even before his sight was restored was Jesus himself. Before, Jesus was someone he had discounted, even ridiculed. But when Jesus appeared to Saul on the road, Saul said, "Who are you, Lord?" (Acts 9:5). Whether or not Saul fully realized that he was hearing the voice of Jesus, we may assume that he knew it was the voice of deity. His use of the term, "Lord," was most likely out of awe and respect for the presence of deity. After Jesus identified himself, Saul offered no argument, but immediately obeyed the commands he had received. He was going to spend the rest of his life understanding what it meant to call Jesus, "Lord."

When Jesus revealed himself to Saul as a living being, Saul had another problem to solve. As a persecutor of the church, we may assume that Saul had ridiculed the report that Jesus had risen from the dead. Perhaps Saul was among those who said the soldiers made up the resurrection story, or the disciples had stolen Jesus' body, or they had gone to the wrong tomb. He may have believed all those things, but on the road to Damascus, he saw for himself that Jesus was alive. He was real. This one vision of Jesus prepared the way for all the other realizations that Saul would have regarding the truth of God. Saul would never have become clear about all these other things if he had not first seen Jesus.

This realization that Jesus is real happened to other people in Scripture, too. I imagine, for instance, that while Judas counted his silver coins of betrayal, he had a sudden realization that he had done something terrible. He ended up taking his life because of that pain. Peter experienced a sudden realization, too. He had declared, "Lord, I am ready to go with you to prison and to death" (Luke 22:33). But during the trial of Jesus when a servant girl said of Peter, "This man was with him," Peter denied with oaths that he even knew Jesus (Luke 22:56-60; Mark 14:69-71). Then a rooster crowed, and he remembered what Jesus said about his denial. A sudden realization.

*Flash*Points

1. How would you describe your experience of realizing that Jesus is not a fairy tale character, but a historical figure who lived and died—and is the Son of God himself?

2. What aspects about Jesus have you been coming to understand better lately (e.g. His humanity, His connectedness with God, His compassion)?

The prodigal son had a sudden realization, too. He spent all of his money on riotous living and then found that he had no friends left either. The only job he could find was feeding the pigs. He got so hungry he began to envy the pigs and wished he could eat what they ate. The Bible says, "he came to himself." (Luke 15:17, KJV). This made him decide to go home—he decided it was better to be a servant in his father's house than to be free in the place he was.

This same sudden realization—coming to one's self—happened to David. He thought he had covered up his sin with Bathsheba until Nathan made him see with blinding clarity that he had sinned against the Lord (2 Samuel 12).

Seeing Ourselves Better

Saul's vision of Jesus made it possible for him to see something else more clearly. He could see himself better. Suddenly he realized, "I'm on the wrong side. I'm on the wrong road. I'm playing for the wrong team." Saul had *always* been zealous for God. He was never a selfish or lazy person. He had been serving God to the best of his knowledge prior to this, but he had gotten it wrong about Jesus. That's a tough thing to recognize. It's always tough to recognize that even though we've been serving the Lord, we've been doing it the wrong way.

Have you ever felt you were not the person you wanted to be—that you hadn't done what you had intended to do with your life? To be disappointed with certain aspects of your life is a painful thing. We can't go back and change the things that we have done or not done. But, like Saul, we also learn that we can become the subjects of forgiveness. For along with the pain of coming to himself came the beautiful message of grace. Saul learned this message well enough that he was able to articulate it effectively for the rest of his life. We can take hold of grace as he did.

Saul also believed. The Bible admonishes us to have faith. After Saul asked, "Who are you, Lord?" he went on to obey. The text says that Saul fasted for three days. Was this a period of mourning for him? A period of repentance? A period of soul-searching? When God used Ananias to restore sight to Saul, the *first* thing he did was be baptized—then he ate and got his strength back. The text also says that "Saul spent several days with the disciples in Damascus. *At once* he began to preach in the synagogues that Jesus is the Son of God" (Acts 9:19, 20). Isn't that amazing? He had been on his way to Damascus to seek out and arrest those "who belonged to the Way," and when he arrived he began preaching in the synagogues that Jesus is the Son of God. Saul wasted no time wallowing in remorse—he began immediately to demonstrate his new priority.

We would do well to follow his example. When we come to Christ, or when we realize that we have been mistaken about one thing or another, why not just pick ourselves up, accept the forgiveness of God, and move forward in His grace? Saul's 360 degree conversion had a high impact on the Jews and Gentiles precisely *because* of his past, and Saul began immediately to use his position as a well-educated, influential man for the Lord's glory. As the Lord told Ananias, "This man is my chosen instrument to carry my name before the Gentiles and their kings and before the people of Israel."

Some people are bothered by the fact that Saul came to know Christ through a vision. They say, "Why doesn't God give all of us a Damascus road experience?" God used extreme measures with Saul because he was a man of extremes. He was stubborn to the point of blindness. Having been raised as a devout Jew and expecting a political messiah instead of a spiritual one, he was not about to accept Jesus as the messiah. We must remember that Saul's rejection of Christianity was not born out of a rejection of God but *because of his faithfulness* as a Jew. He loved God and lived to serve Him, and believed that he was doing that by fighting this new religion. God had to make him "see the light." We must remember too that Jesus performed miracles in order to establish His identity, and God enabled His disciples to perform miracles during the establishment of the church. God gives each of us what we need to make a fair choice. Today we have this record of history and the testimony of countless Christians, besides the evidence of creation that has always existed. We are invited to accept the offer of salvation by hearing the message of grace, believing it, praying, being baptized, and being obedient—exactly as Saul did! And we should!

*Flash*Points

1. In what sort of moments do people see themselves better? In crisis? In the insightful words of a child? In burnout?

2. To which end of the spectrum has God been pulling you lately—to see what you've been doing that needs to be turned around, or, to acknowledge God's grace for your mistakes?

3. In what ways has God been prodding you to "come to yourself"?

4. Of the steps Saul took—taking hold of grace, understanding God in a clearer way, believing God, praying, being baptized—which do you need to do? Some of these "steps" are ongoing—which do you need to do more of?

Saul's ministry was conceived in the moment that he decided to accept God's revelation of truth and put his past behind him. But someone else helped to birth his ministry, someone who could have aborted the ministry before it began.

> In Damascus there was a disciple named Ananias. The Lord called to him in a vision, "Ananias!"
>
> "Yes, Lord," he answered.
>
> The Lord told him, "Go to the house of Judas on Straight Street and ask for a man from Tarsus named Saul, for he is praying. In a vision he has seen a man named Ananias come and place his hands on him to restore his sight."
>
> "Lord," Ananias answered, "I have heard many reports about this man and all the harm he has done to your saints in Jerusalem. And he has come here with authority from the chief priests to arrest all who call on your name."
>
> But the Lord said to Ananias, "Go! This man is my chosen instrument to carry my name before the Gentiles and their kings and before the people of Israel. I will show him how much he must suffer for my name."
>
> But the Lord said to Ananias, "Go! This man is my chosen instrument to carry my name before the Gentiles and their kings and before the people of Israel. I will show him how much he must suffer for my name."
>
> Then Ananias went to the house and entered it. Placing his hands on Saul, he said, "Brother Saul, the Lord—Jesus, who appeared to you on the road as you were coming here—has sent me so that you may see again and be filled with the Holy Spirit." Immediately, something like scales fell from Saul's eyes, and he could see again. He got up and was baptized, and after taking some food, he regained his strength.
>
> Acts 9:10-19

At first, Ananias responded as any of us would. This man, Saul, had the authority to arrest him and have him killed. Even if Ananias wasn't afraid for his own life, his words reveal that he was afraid for the rest of the saints.

Furthermore, this message from the Lord was hard to accept.
Have you ever known anyone who has been a hard-hearted
opponent of God who has turned and become a believer?
Were you skeptical of that person? Did you question their
sincerity, or their trustworthiness? When I think of this kind
of conversion, I think of a story I read recently about George
Wallace, the former governor of Alabama. You may remember that he was known in his earlier days as a proponent of
segregation as well as racism. After he was shot and paralyzed and faced his own struggles, he began to realize what
suffering was like. One day George Wallace wheeled his
chair into the church that had formerly been pastored by
Martin Luther King and asked forgiveness of those he had
once despised. He asked them to forgive the pain he had
caused them—and they did. Wallace dedicated the latter part
of his life to racial reconciliation.

Are you as willing as these African-American Christians
to forgive those who have wronged you in the past? Would
you be able, like Ananias, to bring a formerly antagonistic
person into your fellowship and introduce him as a brother
in Christ? Saul had gone to Damascus to persecute
Christians, but ended up in Damascus as a Christian himself.
This was thanks in large part to the ministry of a man of
courage, named Ananias. He was willing to put his fears and
Saul's past aside, and minister grace to an enemy.
Fortunately for all of us, God is more gracious, more forgiving than we humans tend to be. But we do need to examine
our attitudes towards new believers to see if we are imped-
ing their ministry in any way.

The text says that when Ananias laid his hands on Saul,
"something like scales fell from Saul's eyes" (Acts 9:18). To
the poet in each of us, these physical scales remind us of the
spiritual scales on Saul's eyes. As those spiritual scales fell
off, he could see everything more clearly.

Seeing the Church Better

Saul not only saw Jesus better and saw himself better, but he also saw the church better than he had seen it before. To him, the church had been a bunch of heretics and an object of ridicule. After the vision, he saw the church as something loved by Christ.

It's interesting that when Jesus spoke to Saul, he said, "Saul, why do you persecute me?" What had Saul ever done to Jesus himself? As far as we know, they had never met. Saul didn't put Jesus on the cross (except in the sense that we all put Him there). Jesus' question shows us how personally He takes His relationship to the church. Jesus expressed this same idea when He said, "Whatever you did for one of the least of these brothers of mine, you did for me" (Matthew 25:40). The opposite is true as well. If you hurt the church, you hurt Jesus. Jesus cares for the church as a loving husband and father cares for his family. Saul had once seen the church as his enemy, but he now saw them as friends, supporters, brothers, and sisters.

Seeing Our Mission Better

Through this Damascus road experience, Saul saw his life purpose and direction change. That day Saul saw his mission more clearly than he had ever seen before. He began to see himself as a minister of Christ instead of as an opponent of Christ. He saw himself as a minister to people he had formerly despised. This man who considered himself at the pinnacle of Judaism and a Pharisee of the Pharisees (Acts 23:6, Philippians 3:4-6) started preaching to Gentiles and telling them they could become Christians directly without becoming Jews first. Saul received a lot of opposition and mistreatment for that position, but he stood up for it. Formerly, he would have despised and kept himself from Gentiles, but when he became a Christian, they became his mission.

*Flash*Points

1. Since Jesus takes on the identity of the church personally, that means that we must treat everyone at church the way we want to treat Jesus. That may make us uncomfortable. How difficult is that for you today?
   __ very uncomfortable
   __ better than before
   __ not too bad

2. How has God used loving, courageous individuals to help you see himself or the church more clearly?

3. Try to think of a time in your life when you were headed one direction in your thoughts and behavior and turned around and went the opposite direction. What was that like?

A lot of us have trouble understanding what our mission is. Some people think there is one thing and only one thing that they can do for the Lord. Some discover their mission early in life and others discover it later in life. Some, like Saul, discover it as part of their "mid-life crisis." If any good thing can come out of a mid-life crisis, it is a clarification of your mission in life. I suppose everyone who finds his mission late in life would say, "I would have liked it better if I had submitted earlier."

Ty Cobb is considered by many as the greatest baseball player of all time. He was a great hitter and a great fielder, but he was also one of the meanest players in the history of the game. He did not like other people much. He was even seen sharpening his spikes because he wasn't afraid of injuring people. He lived a life of hedonism—boozing and brawling and getting involved in all kinds of misdeeds. According to an article I read, he found Christ as he was dying. He said to a friend, "Tell the boys I have found Christ and I regret waiting until the bottom of the ninth. I wish I had found him in the first inning."

If you missed finding your way to Christ or didn't find your mission until late in life, don't despair. You can come to Christ now as Saul did that day on the road to Damascus. Saul's vision motivated him for the rest of his life. I don't want to play amateur psychologist two thousand years after an event, but I wonder if Paul didn't feel responsible for doing a lot of harm to the church. He knew he had been saved by grace, but perhaps regret for his former misdeeds was part of his motivation for all the great things that he went on to do. Perhaps his past helped him accept all the hardships that came, for every hardship he placed on somebody else, he eventually received himself.

If there is some pain in your life or something in your past that you're not proud of, God can use it to minister to other people. I'm not saying that you should serve the Lord out of guilt, but that God can take whatever has happened to us and bring something good out of it, as He did for Saul.

The story of Saul's conversion and his subsequent ministry has inspired a lot of people throughout history, including Augustine. Augustine read Paul's account, saw himself, and came to love Christ. Paul's story inspired Martin Luther to change his mission in life and to give it over to Christ and his ministry.

Another hero of church history affected by Paul's ministry was John Wesley, founder of the Methodist church. John Wesley grew up as a young man of privilege. He attended the finest school, Oxford University, and earned a master's degree there. He decided he wanted to become a missionary to the American Indians, so he signed on to go to the Georgia colony in America. As he crossed the ocean, a great storm came up and Wesley feared for his life. Also on the ship were some Moravians, who exhibited great peace in spite of the horrific danger. This troubled Wesley, and he wrote in his journal, "I have come to America to evangelize the Indians, but who is going to evangelize me?"

While John Wesley was in Georgia, he had many disagreements with the leaders, so he went back to England thinking himself a terrible failure. He kept remembering those Moravians, however, and how much he respected them. One night he went into a little Moravian chapel in Aldersgate. The regular preacher wasn't there, so one of the laymen got up and read from Martin Luther's commentary on Romans.

Now that book is a snoozer if there ever was one, but Wesley was ready that night to hear what Luther was saying and what Paul was saying. He later described how that night he felt his heart strangely warmed within him. That night, John Wesley found his mission. He decided he would preach to the poor, to the coal miners and to the outcasts of society. He became an itinerant evangelist and spoke to crowds of thousands. This fervor eventually produced a great religious movement.

That would not have happened if John Wesley hadn't opened himself up one night to a sudden realization. This man of privilege found his mission among the poor. Consider that. No wonder Wesley felt such kinship to the apostle Paul's turnaround experience. Wesley had always wanted to serve God and do what God wanted him to do, and in Aldersgate he found his particular purpose and mission.

Wesley never looked back and Paul never looked back. Paul dreamed about going to Rome and he did. Then in Rome he dreamed of going to Spain. We don't know whether he made it or not, but he was always looking ahead to the next town, the next village, and the next church—all because of an event one day on the road to Damascus. On that physical road Saul was given a new spiritual road to travel. When he testified later about this event, he said to the King Agrippa, "I was not disobedient to the vision from heaven" (Acts 26:19). That's an important message for us to hear. For when we do receive our vision, however it may come to us, we dare not be disobedient to it.

*Flash*Points

1. How can we use regret to refocus instead of letting it eat us up?

2. Who has been a memorable, penetrating influence on you as the Moravians were on John Wesley?

3. One of the keys to finding our mission in life is embodied in this statement from above: "If there is some pain in your life or something in your past that you're not proud of, God can use it to minister to other people." What has occurred in your life that God is leading you to use for His glory?

You can't expect to hear a voice as Saul did, and you may not be put under God's spotlight as Saul was. But somehow, some way, the Lord Jesus will communicate with you. You will have an opportunity to say, "Here I am, Lord," or not to say it. You'll need to decide whether you are going to follow God's way or not. God may put you on a different road and, if He does, it will change your life, and your destination.